MANAGING THE METROLOGY SYSTEM

SECOND EDITION

Also available from ASQ Quality Press

Reliability, Maintainability, and Availability Assessment, Second Edition
Mitchell O. Locks

Failure Mode and Effect Analysis: FMEA From Theory to Execution
D. H. Stamatis

Weibull Analysis
Bryan Dodson

Glossary and Tables for Statistical Quality Control, Third Edition
ASQ Statistics Division

Statistical Process Control Methods for Long and Short Runs, Second Edition
Gary K. Griffith

SPC Essentials and Productivity Improvement: A Manufacturing Approach
William A. Levinson and Frank Tumbelty

To request a complimentary catalog of publications, call 800-248-1946.

Managing the Metrology System

Second Edition

C. Robert Pennella

ASQ Quality Press
Milwaukee, Wisconsin

Managing the Metrology System, second edition
C. R. Pennella

Library of Congress Cataloging-in-Publication Data

Pennella, C. Robert
  Managing the metrology system/C. Robert Pennella.—2nd ed.
    p. cm.
  Includes bibliographical references and index.
  ISBN 0-87389-421-9 (alk. paper)
  1. Engineering inspection.   2. Mensuration.   3. Quality control.
I. Title.
TS156.2.P46   1997   97-10667
658.5'68—dc21   CIP

ISBN 0-87389-421-9

Acquisitions Editor: Roger Holloway
Project Editor: Jeannie Bohn

ASQ Mission: The American Society for Quality advances individual and organizational performance excellence worldwide by providing opportunities for learning, quality improvement, and knowledge exchange.

Attention: Schools and Corporations
ASQ Quality Press books, audiotapes, videotapes, and software are available at quantity discounts with bulk purchases for business, educational, or instructional use. For information, please contact ASQ Quality Press at 800-248-1946, or write to ASQ Quality Press, P.O. Box 3005, Milwaukee, WI 53201-3005.

For a free copy of the ASQ Quality Press Publications Catalog, including ASQ membership information, call 800-248-1946.

Printed in the United States of America

∞ Printed on acid-free paper

American Society for Quality

611 East Wisconsin Avenue
P.O. Box 3005
Milwaukee, Wisconsin 53201-3005

To my wife, Anita.
Thanks for the understanding,
support, and love.

CONTENTS

CHAPTER 7

Costs Associated with Metrology Systems Management   131

PREFACE

In a rapidly changing world, it sometimes seems that measurement and standards are a haven of objectivity amidst the chaos of subjective opinion. Yet the standards that surround the subject of calibration as they affect quality often leave suppliers thumbing through pages of jargon and lost in confusion. After a career in the field of quality, one lesson stands out. People will address quality issues when they have a clear picture of the actions and systems required to run a first-class quality and measurement operation. Conversely, when terminology and procedures are nebulous, energy that should be spent on implementation is lost on research, confusion, and frustration.

The first edition of this book addressed the need of the supplier and his/her technical staff by providing a step-by-step system for establishing, maintaining, and documenting an effective calibration system. The book clarified the critical relationship of calibration to total quality management and identified both the mistakes that suppliers can find by measuring properly and those mistakes, or errors of omission, that are often overlooked until a crisis makes these errors all too obvious. This section, which is addressed in chapter 1, has been enhanced by relating its message to the state-of-the-art techniques for planning and managing calibration systems as part of a cost effective-quality program.

The "how to" of setting up and auditing an effective calibration system appears in chapters 2 and 3. The reader will find a step-by-step system with examples and sample documents that can be quickly adapted to the specific requirements of his/her work setting. This chapter connects its recommendations to the American National Standards Institute (ANSI), the International Organization for Standardization (ISO), and the American Society for Quality Control (ASQC) Q9000 standards. This edition helps the reader who is making a transition from the U.S. Government-published standard known as the MIL–STD 45662A Calibration System. This edition will also enhance the reader's efforts to become ISO certified or to adopt ISO-standards. Since 1987, when the International Organization for Standardization (ISO) introduced quality standards in concert with the American National Standards Institute and the American Society for Quality Control, businesses have been able to save money and improve results by achieving ISO supplier certification and registration. The reader will find that the application of the information in chapters 2 and 3 will contribute to those cost savings by reducing redundant effort and by capitalizing on proper preparation to support current or future ISO efforts.

Chapters 6 and 7 have been added to this edition. These chapters will assist the calibration professional to document capabilities and working procedures more effectively. The reader will be able to adapt the sample quality system manual in chapter 6 for use in documenting and clarifying calibration procedures. Chapter 7 helps the metrology professional to adapt better methods to communicate the advantage of management's investment in the right human and technological resources to support an affective metrology program and demonstrates ways that correct calibration decisions can positively affect the bottom line.

ANSI/ISO/ASQC Q9001 and Q9002 quality system standards do not specifically require the maintenance and use of quality cost data as a management element of a quality system program. However, chapter 7 "Costs Associated with Metrology Management," is added to the second edition in deference to those suppliers who elect to tailor their quality system manual to accommodate cost of metrology data collection.

In summary, this book will help quality technicians and other supplier and customer personnel to readily recognize and establish a quality program with an emphasis on practical application. The integration of calibration into the scheme of a total quality system will help to ensure not only the integrity of the total system but also contribute to the strength of the company's reputation, good will, and profitability.

This book is a labor that reflects the help and support of many people. The layout for the book's graphics were done by the skilled hands of Joan Wyndrum. I owe an ongoing debt of appreciation to Rosemary F. Garvey, the president of Blanchette Tool and Gage Manufacturing Company. Her willingness and ability to share her knowledge of the practical application of quality systems serves the profession well and has helped me greatly over the years. Editing and formatting help was provided by my colleague, Donna I. Mugavero, a gifted problem solver and ever a clear thinker. I am most grateful for the inspiration, sage critique, and guidance provided by Dr. Michael A. Pennella, who is not only an able writer but also a great son.

Finally, I acknowledge my colleagues and friends in the American Society for Quality Control (ASQC), notably Frank Corcoran, Fred DeNude, and other members of the North Jersey Section for their commitment to a strong profession.

C. Robert Pennella
January, 1997

FIGURES

CHAPTER 1

Overview

The proper application of a calibration system is one of the most important areas in which quality-assurance personnel can positively effect the low quality and high costs associated with poorly manufactured products. Conversely, when a calibration system is ignored or improperly implemented, suppliers of goods and services can encounter a tarnished reputation at best and, potentially, financial disaster.

A properly implemented calibration system is the foundation of the inspection systems and quality programs that support total quality management (TQM) strategy for the following reasons:

- Measurement confidence can only be achieved through the use of instruments of known accuracy.
- The accuracy requirements of measuring and test equipment (M&TE) are imperative to the corrective active action process aimed at the causes of nonconforming products.

- Process capability techniques cannot be used to full advantage unless M&TE and related measurements are reliable from the start.

PROJECT SIXTY

In the early 1960s the U.S. government conducted a study entitled "Project Sixty" to evaluate the feasibility of relying on the "inspection system concept" to determine the adequacy of supplies and/or services prior to their submission for acceptance by the supplier or customer's quality-assurance representative. The objective of this concept was to assure adequate quality throughout all areas of contract performance: planning, work instruction, fabrication, assembly, inspection, testing, storage, and shipping.

"Project Sixty" was put into service in 1965 with the support of U.S. Secretary of Defense Robert McNamara. Both the government and the private sector recognized that it was not only more economical but also more effective to establish and maintain an acceptable quality-control system than to rely on end-item inspection to control product quality. The "Project Sixty" concept initially focused on defect detection but later relied on defect-prevention processes through the application of TQM principles based on the work of Dr. W. Edwards Deming and others.

The transition to preventive strategies was brought about by several factors. It was evident that no production or inspection system could be perfect and that not even 100 percent inspection of every item, as prevalent in the past, could preclude the acceptance of some defective supplies. Also, since the number of quality-assurance personnel that could be placed in a supplier's plant was small in comparison to the number of production personnel, the task of end-item inspection proved to be monumental.

Hence, today heavy reliance is necessarily placed upon continuous process improvement, the hallmark of TQM. M&TE of known accuracy plays an important role in verifying the adequacy of relevant processes that lead to quality products and services.

EVALUATION PROCESS

To maximize the effectiveness of a supplier's inspection system or quality program, as well as support the objectives of TQM, all aspects of the metrology program must be carefully and continuously evaluated. If continuous calibration process improvement is to be achieved, this evaluation process requires careful attention to those policies, procedures, and processes that lead to improved products and services.

Three decision-making factors affect the successful application of calibration policies and procedures. Each must be carefully considered and included in management planning.

1. *Timely actions*   The quality-assurance process should be timely, all-inclusive, and unbiased. The timely review of contract quality and product design requirements will

- Eliminate any oversights that might lead to the production of nonconforming products
- Establish processes that lead to continuous product/service improvements
- Eliminate the presence of potential errors of omission
- Address the delivery constraints of the customer
- Reinforce the quality expectations of the customer

2. *Unbiased decisions*   To maximize the quality effort and to assure that the objectives of TQM are met, management must ensure that unbiased decisions are made regarding the policies and procedures and product design requirements that lead to the calibration processes.

Decisions influenced by bias prevail when personnel fail to adhere to established processes. When policies and procedures are acceptable from the outset and are applied without undue subjectivity, the objectives of good quality will be met. However, when attention to details goes astray, good quality will also go astray. Sustained attention to established standards will greatly reduce biased conditions as well as reduce errors of omission.

Data used to evaluate the adequacy of process capabilities will be biased when the information represents an opinion of an individual rather than representing the intent of established written instructions. For example:

- The calibration technician calibrates M&TE under ambient conditions rather than under environmental conditions established by written instructions.
- The calibration technician arbitrarily decides to extend established calibration intervals even though the calibration history indicates that this course of action is not justified.
- The calibration technician arbitrarily modifies calibration procedures without justification when calibrating M&TE, rather than following the instructions furnished in specific documented calibration procedures.
- Biased conditions are effected by human errors. Human errors effect the application of a metrology system not only by what is done but also by what is overlooked. The sources of biased errors are threefold.
  a. Instrument accuracy requirements
  b. Calibration system description
  c. Errors of omission

3. *All inclusive*   When management policy and procedures ensure that timely, comprehensive, and unbiased decisions are being made, success for the quality system shifts to the instruments used for measuring.

The accuracy requirements of M&TE play an important role in the accumulation of meaningful data. However, the calibration data that are generated are only as good as the reliability of the measuring equipment. Therefore, when measurements are made with measuring equipment of unknown accuracy, the quality of the data that are generated deteriorates.

The critical role of instrument accuracy is covered under the following topics:

- The adequacy of measurement standards (MS) and M&TE
- The importance of higher-level accuracy ratios between MS and M&TE
- The method of selecting the best MS and M&TE for desired calibrations

- The impact that out-of-tolerance conditions have on instrument accuracy
- The traceability of M&TE to measurement standards of known accuracy

CALIBRATION SYSTEM DESCRIPTION

The objective of this book is to provide a step-by-step procedure for designing and implementing an effective and efficient metrology system that supports TQM by calibrating M&TE and using MS of known accuracy.

The step-by-step description of a calibration system is intended to guide you through the establishment and maintenance of a calibration system. It is supported by "Metrology Audits." Two case studies are also provided to demonstrate practical application of the calibration system. The first case study describes actions taken by a supplier with unknown calibration system capabilities. The second case study provides a generic example of a supplier's calibration system that can be used as an example for the development of calibration system documentation. ANSI/ISO/ASQC Q9001 and Q9002 quality system standards do not specifically require the maintenance and use of quality cost data yet many suppliers are concerned with these costs as a measure of their effectiveness. The ability of those involved with calibration to reduce cost while improving quality is addressed in chapter 7.

The type of calibration system that a supplier must put into effect is dependent, of course, upon the complexity of the product design, contract quality requirements, and customer expectations. There are, however, some generic requirements that a supplier should be aware of from the outset of planning the calibration system.

CATEGORIES OF CONTRACT QUALITY REQUIREMENTS

Contract quality requirements fall into three general categories depending on the extent of quality assurance needed.[1] Knowing the differences among these categories plays an important part in establishing a calibration system that will be acceptable to both customer and supplier.

1. Under Category 1, reliance on inspection is placed solely on the supplier wherein there is no requirement for participation in the quality-assurance process at the supplier's plant by the customer. This category normally applies to common/noncomplex items.

2. Category 2 is known as standard inspection requirements. This category requires the supplier to have an inspection system that is acceptable to the customer. It neither specifies a requirement for the application of a specific inspection system nor a calibration standard. Normally the selected inspection system and related calibration system requirement are determined by the supplier. This category applies to noncomplex/noncritical items.

3. Category 3, which will be dealt with in this book, is known as higher-level contract quality requirements.

    • The detailed information that is required for the application of Category 3, higher-level contract quality requirements, which involve complex-critical items, is contained in chapter 2, "Calibration System Description."

    • Where it is in the customer's interest that higher-level contract quality requirements be maintained, the contract shall require the prime contractor, and/or his/her delegated subcontractor, to comply with ANSI/ISO/ASQC Q9001-1994, *Quality Systems—Model for Quality Assurance in Design, Development, Production, Installation, and Servicing;* or ANSI/ISO/ASQC Q9002-1994, *Quality Systems—Model for Quality Assurance in Production, Installation, and Servicing.*

    • When higher-level contract quality requirements apply, the contract or purchase order shall require the supplier to comply with a calibration system that is normally referenced in the quality program or inspection system standard.

- In some instances, the calibration system requirement may be referenced separate from the quality program or inspection system standard. This action is taken by the purchaser when other than higher-level contract quality requirements are specified.

Today many of the calibration system standards that were introduced to the public by the Department of Defense over the past five decades are being replaced by standards published by the American National Standards Institute (ANSI), the American Society for Quality Assurance (ASQC), the International Organization for Standardization (ISO), the International Electromechanical Commission (IEC), and the National Conference of Standards Laboratories (NCSL). A representative example of these standards includes: (a) ANSI/ASQC M1, *American National Standard for Calibration Systems,* (b) ISO/IEC Guide 25, *General Requirements for the Competence of Calibration and Testing,* (c) ANSI/NCSL Z540-1, *Calibration Laboratories and Measuring and Test Equipment—General Requirements,* and (d) ISO 10012-1, *Quality Assurance Requirements for Measuring Equipment—Part 1: Measuring Equipment.*

Each supplier functions individually, and consequently the calibration system of each supplier may differ in specific method.

Each standard presents certain basic functional concepts of a calibration system so as to assure that M&TE are sufficiently accurate to ensure supply or service conformance to contractual requirements. For example, calibration requirements that involve Category 1 and Category 2 (noncomplex, noncritical items) will not require an elaborate calibration system because of the loose tolerances of the items offered to the customer. The supplier will require lower accuracy levels of measuring equipment for these items. In addition, intervals of calibration will be less frequent than those required for complex-critical items, and policies and procedures are minimal in comparison to Category 3 items.

Category 3 items involve all of the elements of a calibration system. These types of items have tighter product tolerances, calibration intervals that are more frequent than Category 1 and 2 items, and policies and procedures that are more elaborate.

THE IMPORTANCE OF ESTABLISHING A CONSISTENT CALIBRATION SYSTEM

To assure uniformity of understanding and to assure continuity of satisfactory operations when personnel changes occur, all proposed or existing calibration procedures should be documented. Without written guides, policy and procedural questions are bound to arise and variations in practice that occur will result in confusion and uncertainty. Having a documented calibration system in place in the early stages of contract and technical review provides the supplier and those responsible for calibration with significant advantages. The supplier as well as the customer's quality-assurance representatives can complete their assigned functions by understanding and agreeing upon the type of calibration required. The chapters that follow describe the steps that a supplier should take to establish such a system for consistent calibration. The establishment of a consistent calibration system does more than prescribe what is to be done to produce a quality product the right way every time, it establishes a system to avoid the unseen errors that manifest themselves in what is often unwritten in contracts, job descriptions, and often occur not based on what someone does but what he/she overlooks. These are the errors of omission.

Calibration system standards, like most other specifications, have inherent subjective characteristics. Standards specify *what* controls are to be implemented. It is the user's responsibility to define *how* the standard applies to products and/or services as well as *how* the requirements will be implemented. Therefore, a supplier must *not* fall into the trap of performing a cursory review of the contract quality requirements and product design requirements. Experience has shown that when this course of action is taken, errors of omission usually follow.

When potential errors of omission are prevalent, the adequacy of a calibration system will become suspect, staff application will be questioned, and quality costs will be augmented. Errors of omission become evident when necessary procedures or work instructions are left undone or when established processes and/or work instructions are not implemented. Errors of omission are minimized when a quality program, a TQM master plan, and an associated calibration system receive the support and commitment of management. This support is essential if

1. *The objectives of a calibration system are to be achieved.* The objectives of calibration systems management are maximized only when contract quality requirements are clearly defined between the purchaser and his/her advisor(s). This is an imperative for meeting the needs and interests of the supplier as well as meeting the customer's needs and expectations. A clearly defined contract and associated technical documents are also an imperative for management and operations personnel who hope to produce a product or services in accordance with contract quality requirement and with inspection, measuring, and test equipment of known accuracy.

2. *The quality expectations of the customer are to be satisfied.* Satisfaction of customer expectations is achieved when contract quality requirements are free from errors, ambiguity, and/or omissions and specified requirements are clearly defined in a supplier's quality plan.

3. *Reduced quality costs are to be achieved.*   When technical requirements are clearly defined, suppliers of products and services will be able to meet contract requirements correctly the first time. They will also be in a favorable position to implement policy, procedures, and processes that are cost effective.

The following are pertinent topics (quality elements) as well as potential omission factors that pertain to a calibration system and the impact they have on the objectives of good quality when they are left undone or not implemented.

  1. Planning process
    a. Omission factors:
      • Prompt review of contract quality requirements
      • Identification of inspection and testing requirements
      • Required resources

    b. Impact: Failure to review, identify, and summarize contract quality and product design requirements to assure that there is a clear understanding of technical requirements, and failure to consider personnel, equipment, and facility requirements might jeopardize contract performance and delivery schedules and lead to unnecessary quality costs.

2. Organizational structure

    a. Omission factors:
- Authority
- Responsibility

    b. Impact: Failure to establish responsibilities and authority will undermine the objectives of good management as well as employee morale. It might also compromise the quality assurance expectations of the customer.

3. Contract administration

    a. Omission factors:
- Availability of pertinent technical data package
- Supplementary contract quality requirements
- Specifications
- Drawings

    b. Impact: The contract administrator must ensure that the complete technical data are made available to engineering, production, and quality-assurance personnel for their planning and implementation. The timely review of drawings, specifications, and other contract quality requirements is necessary to
- Clear up any vague or ambiguous language or settle differences of opinion between the supplier and the customer prior to the start of production
- Assure that all contract quality requirements have been considered
- Determine that all operations will be cost-effective
- Verify that delivery schedules are met

4. Detail contract and purchase-order requirements

    a. Omission factors:
- Review
- Summarize

- Document
- Implement

b. Impact: Failure of the quality-control manager or a designated representative to perform an in-depth review of specified requirements may result in
- Noncompliance with all specified requirements
- Customer complaints
- Delay in delivery schedules
- Unnecessary added costs
- Possible loss of repeat business

5. Policy procedures

a. Omission factor:
- All of the applicable elements required of a calibration system

b. Impact: The preparation of policy procedures is required to support calibration processes. The absence of documented procedures will impede the substantiation of product quality and deter the objectives of process capability studies.

6. Product/service verification stations

a. Omission factor:
- In-house and off-site product and calibration verification stations

b. Impact: Identifying inspection stations facilitates the planning processes for the type and amount of calibration, inspection, and testing activity that will be required at the respective station.

7. Control of purchases

a. Omission factors:
- Supplier capability
- Supplier performance
- Audits
- Feedback data

b. Impact:
- When a proposed supplier's capabilities are unknown, the contractor should evaluate the supplier's qualifications prior to issuing a purchase order.

- A supplier with proven capabilities must substantiate its capabilities by furnishing ongoing objective evidence regarding quality assurance operations.
- When controls are not established and implemented, there will be no assurance that required quality assurance capabilities are adequately maintained.

8. Control of M&TE and MS

   a. Omission factors:
   - Adequacy and availability of M&TE and MS
   - Policy procedures
   - System maintenance
   - Control of customer-furnished M&TE
   - Control of company-designed M&TE
   - Support to the purchasing manager
   - Calibration intervals
   - Traceability of MS and M&TE
   - Calibration status
   - Calibration audits

   b. Impact:
   - The absence of some or all of the elements that comprise a written calibration system will lead to conditions that adversely affect the establishment, maintenance, and control of product quality and production capabilities.
   - Accuracies of M&TE and MS must be verified with higher-level standards if the integrity of production processes is to be maintained.
   - If the calibration system is to be cost-effective, it must provide satisfactory provisions for maintaining M&TE and MS that are used in-house as well as by subcontractors.
   - The calibration system must also establish a procedure early in the system that will identify significant out-of-tolerance conditions.

9. Corrective action

   a. Omission factors:
   - Correction of assignable causes

- Adequacy of corrective action
- Correction of unfavorable trends
- Follow-up action regarding the adequacy of corrective action

b. Impact:
- The calibration system must provide for early detection and correction of reported out-of-tolerance conditions.
- Failure to take immediate corrective action might lead to additional staff hours and added cost.

10. Records

a. Omission factors:
- Accuracy
- Completeness
- Reliability
- Nature of observation
- Number of observations
- Type and number of deficiencies
- Corrective action taken
- Monitoring of recorded information
- Analysis of records

b. Impact:
- The absence of objective records will impede the objectives of good management.
- The collection, review, and analysis of objective records are necessary to measure the effectiveness of a supplier's calibration system as well as to indicate the supplier's calibration capabilities.

11. Storage and handling

a. Omission factors:
- Handling practices
- Packaging and transportation
- Storage of M&TE and MS

b. Impact: Without a procedure to control the storage, handling, and transportation of M&TE and MS, the user may doubt the accuracy of the measuring equipment as well as the instruments' control and maintenance.

RESPONSIBILITIES

Responsibility does not end with in-plant metrology actions. A supplier must also assure that the accuracy of all measurements and calibration functions performed by outside sources that affect quality or conformance, such as at an independent laboratory or at a subcontractor's plant, are effectively controlled.

This need not result in complete uniformity or standardization of calibration policies or procedures between the contractor and subcontractor; the controls placed on the subcontractor, however, should satisfy the requirements established by the procurement document. It is important to note that most functions of the calibration system are usually performed by the prime contractor; the purchase agreement between the customer and supplier, therefore, should focus only on those services that the prime contractor has elected to be performed by an outside source.

The responsibility for managing the metrology system is usually divided among

- The quality control manager
- The quality engineer
- The metrology manager
- The calibration technician

Some small companies cannot afford the expense associated with a full staff of managers. Under these conditions, all or most of the responsibilities are shared by the quality-control manager and the calibration technician.

Other companies utilize the full services of an independent calibration laboratory. Some may use an independent calibration laboratory to perform just a portion of the functions of the established calibration system, such as calibrating measurement standards or repairing some instruments.

Do not overlook the fact that the prime contractor is responsible to customers for the quality functions performed by subcontractors. It is important, therefore, to ensure a clear understanding between the prime contractor and the subcontractor regarding calibration requirements imposed on the subcontractor. This clarity is usually stated in the purchase agreement and, when necessary, during a postaward conference between the prime contractor and subcontractor.

PLANNING FOR THE APPLICATION OF A CALIBRATION SYSTEM

The questions to consider during the planning process are threefold.

1. *What are the tightest product tolerances allowed for products and services offered?* The satisfactory identification and control of the tightest product tolerance will provide positive indications that other products with looser tolerances will be adequately controlled.

2. *What kind of calibration equipment is needed to check the product and M&TE?* Due consideration should be given to the accuracy level of the M&TE and MS that are required to check the product. A high accuracy ratio between the comparator and the item being checked will reduce potential measurement error.

3. *Will there be a need to solicit the services of an independent calibration laboratory to perform all or part of the calibration processes?* If the answer is yes, and if the suggested source is one with unknown calibration capabilities, the supplier must evaluate the capabilities of those potential outside sources prior to issuing a purchase order for required services.

DOCUMENTATION

Documentation is another important function of the calibration process. Without it, the selection of the required MS and M&TE may be compromised. Timely documentation of calibration requirements, when coordinated with inspection and testing requirements, will preclude the inadvertent omission of contract quality requirements and at the same time enhance the quality expectations of the customer.

MANAGEMENT SUPPORT

All of the topics that we will cover in this book will not work unless the supplier specifies its position regarding the importance of measuring equipment of known accuracy. For example, not too long ago a study was made on comparable M&TE between two companies. One company had established and maintained a documented calibration system, while the other company elected to recalibrate its equipment only when it was found to be unreliable. The results of the study conclusively showed that the cost per unit to calibrate only when M&TE was found to be unreliable was much greater than the cost of maintaining a documented calibration system through proper training and management. Hence, proper planning supported by documented policies and procedures rather than a crisis-only reaction will produce a calibration operation that excels and a business that is profitable.

Notes

1. U.S. Department of Defense, General Services Administration, and National Aeronautics and Space Administration: *Federal Acquisition Regulation (FAR)*, 1995, Part 46, Clause 46.202.

CHAPTER 2

Calibration System Description

Systems consist of elements working together to create an effective and efficient whole. Systems may consist of procedures, departments, manual and automated processes, or other elements that can be isolated and analyzed independently and in relation to other elements. Accordingly, a calibration system consists of several elements that, when understood, can produce dividends for a contractor and its customers.

Calibration systems meet two objectives:

1. To provide the customer with an indication of a supplier's calibration capabilities
2. To reduce quality costs through the early detection of nonconforming products and processes with the use of measuring equipment of known accuracy

The basic elements of a calibration system include:

- Responsibilities
- Planning processes
- Environmental controls
- Intervals of calibration
- Calibration procedures
- Adequacy of measurement standards and inspection, measuring, and test equipment
- Out-of-tolerance conditions
- Calibration sources
- Application of records
- Calibration status
- Control of subcontractor calibration
- Storage and handling
- Maintenance of policies and procedures

Several standards exist that set requirements for the establishment, implementation, and continuous control of the accuracy of inspection, measuring, and test equipment. These standards specify criteria that, when met, will be compatible to both the customer and supplier. Examples of such standards include:

1. ANSI/ASQC M1, 1987, American National Standard for Calibration Systems   This standard specifies general requirements for the quality of calibration in accordance with established practices or objective quality-control techniques. This standard delineates the requirements for systems to calibrate measuring instruments to specified accuracies; it is intended to cover only the operations engaged in the calibration of measuring instruments.[1]

2. ISO/IEC Guide 25, 1990, General Requirements for the Competence of Calibration and Testing Laboratories   This guide sets out general requirements in accordance with which a laboratory has to demonstrate that it operates without error if it is to be recognized to carry out specific calibrations or tests.[2] Additional requirements and information that have to be disclosed for assessing competence or for determining competence with other criteria may be specified by the organization or authority granting the recognition (or approval), depending upon the specific character of the task of the laboratory.[3]

3. *ANSI/NCSL Z 540-1, 1994, Calibration Laboratories and Measuring and Test Equipment—General Requirements* Part 1 of this standard sets out the general requirements in accordance with which a calibration laboratory must demonstrate that it operates if it is to be recognized as competent to carry out specific calibrations. Part 1 applies to calibration laboratories in the development and implementation of their quality systems.[4] Part II of this standard sets out quality assurance for a supplier's system to control the accuracy of the M&TE used to assure that supplies and services comply with prescribed requirements.[5] The role of the purchaser in monitoring a supplier's compliance with requirements of this standard may be fulfilled by a third party, such as an accredited or certification body.[6]

4. *ISO 10012-1, 1992, Quality Assurance Requirements for Measuring Equipment—Part 1: Metrological Confirmation System for Measuring Equipment* This part of ISO 10012 contains quality requirements for a supplier to ensure that measurements are made with the intended accuracy. It also contains guidance on the implementation of the requirements and specifies the main feature of the confirmation system to be used for a supplier's equipment.[7,8] The section is applicable to measuring equipment used in the demonstration of compliance with a specification but does not apply to other items of measuring equipment. This part of ISO 10012 does not deal exclusively with other elements that may affect measurement results such as methods of measurement, competence of personnel, and so on; these are dealt with more specifically in other international standards.[9]

It is important to note that it is not the intent of these standards to stereotype calibration system requirements among individual suppliers. Their primary purpose is to present basic concepts which, when properly implemented, will allow a supplier to develop, implement, and maintain a calibration system that is tailored

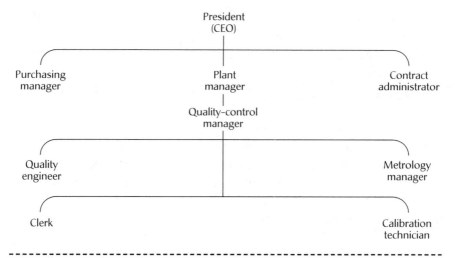

Figure 2.1   A typical organizational structure.

to meet specific needs and expectations relating to a purchase agreement between first and second parties associated with products and/or services solicited or offered.

ELEMENTS OF A CALIBRATION SYSTEM
Organizational Structure

The analysis of a calibration system, like many other production issues that influence quality, begins with an understanding of the organization. Clear lines of communication, responsibility, and reporting enhance the capabilities of the contractor to effectively establish and, more importantly, carry out calibration responsibilities. The organizational structure is beneficial when it is depicted, as a minimum, with hierarchical relationships apparent (see Figure 2.1).

Responsibilities

The responsibilities of the metrology department include the following:

* Preparation of the calibration system description
* Preparation or acquisition of calibration procedures

- Control of the system
- Calibration of measuring equipment
- Identification and correction of out-of-tolerance conditions
- Control of customer-furnished measuring equipment
- Performance of calibration audits
- Support of the purchasing manager
- Control and maintenance of company-designed measuring equipment
- Maintenance of calibration records
- Compliance with established calibration frequencies
- Proper storage and handling of M&TE

Responsibilities for managing the metrology system are normally divided among quality-assurance personnel as follows:

Function	Responsible individual(s)
Policy procedures (system description)	Quality-control manager and/or a designated representative
Calibration procedures	Quality-control manager and/or a designated representative
Control of the system	Quality-control manager
Calibration of equipment	Metrology department and/or an independent calibration laboratory
Correction of out-of-tolerance conditions	Quality-control manager and/or a designated representative
Control of customer-furnished equipment	Calibration technician as required by contract requirements
Calibration audits	Quality-control manager or a designated representative
Support to the purchasing manager	Quality-control manager
Company-designed measuring equipment	Quality-control manager with support from quality engineering

Maintenance of calibration records	Calibration technician
Compliance with established calibration frequencies	Calibration technician
Storage and handling	Calibration technician and the user of the instruments

Planning

The planning process begins with a prompt review of the proposed contract (solicitation), the contract award, and the technical-data package. If there is ambiguity or if differences of opinion exist between the customer and the supplier concerning contract quality requirements and if clarification cannot be accomplished via telephone or correspondence, then a postaward conference between the supplier and customer quality-assurance representatives may be required. A postaward orientation aids both customer and supplier to (1) achieve a clear and mutual understanding of all contract requirements and (2) identify and resolve potential problems.[10]

When contract quality requirements are established and made known to the quality-control manager by the contract administrator, inspection and calibration planning can begin. One recommended method for communicating contract quality requirements is to establish a master requirements list. The list is prepared for each product or assembly and requires modification only when there are significant changes to the product design or other contract quality requirements (see Figures 2.2 and 2.3).

Environmental Controls

There are three factors to consider when determining the required extent of environmental controls.

1. The accuracy of measurement standards
2. The accuracy of M&TE
3. The product tolerances

1. Date _____

2. Part name _____   3. Part number _____

4. Characteristic code number	5. Characteristic identification	6. Measuring device (MD)	7. MD identification number	8. MD code number
_____	_____	_____	_____	_____
_____	_____	_____	_____	_____
_____	_____	_____	_____	_____
_____	_____	_____	_____	_____
_____	_____	_____	_____	_____
_____	_____	_____	_____	_____
_____	_____	_____	_____	_____
_____	_____	_____	_____	_____

9. Prepared by   10. Title   11. Date

_____   _____   _____

Figure 2.2   Master requirements list.

When there is a clear understanding of instrument accuracy as well as product tolerance requirements, a determination can be made regarding the extent of environmental controls. Establishing environmental controls eliminates potential detrimental conditions that may affect the accuracy and stability of M&TE and MS. The environmental elements that affect instrument accuracy include

- Temperature
- Relative humidity
- Dust (particle count)
- Electrical and radio frequency noise
- Lighting

Block number	**Action**
1. Date	Enter as appropriate.
2. Part name	Enter the name of the product that is to be inspected.
3. Part number	Enter the product part number.
4. Characteristic code number	a. Enter drawing dimension code number.
	b. When a specification applies, enter the applicable specification paragraph number or its code number.
	c. When special contract quality requirements apply, enter the applicable contract section paragraph or its code number.
5. Characteristic identification	Enter all of the product parameters.
	a. For drawings, enter actual dimensions.
	b. For specifications, enter specification number, applicable section, and paragraph number.
	c. For special contract quality requirements, enter contract section and paragraph number.
6. Measuring device (MD)	Enter the instrument that will be used to check the respective characteristic.
7. MD identification number	Enter the identification number assigned to the measuring instrument.
8. MD code number	Enter the code number (assigned by the quality-control manager or a designated representative) that identifies the measuring instrument.
	This number traces nonconforming products and/or measuring equipment when married with the respective product inspection report.
9. Prepared by	Enter the name of the quality-control manager or a designated representative.
10. Title	Enter as appropriate.
11. Date	Enter as appropriate.

Figure 2.3 Instructions for preparing the master requirements list.

INTERVALS OF CALIBRATION

Measuring equipment should be calibrated as often as necessary to maintain prescribed accuracies. Calibrations may be accomplished on an established frequency or prior to use. Where there is sporadic production, the "prior to use" method is recommended. When production is continuous, the establishment of calibration frequencies (intervals) is recommended. Calibration frequencies are usually assigned by one of the following:

1. A supplier's calibration laboratory   Calibration intervals are normally established within a company's own calibration laboratory by a metrology manager or his/her designated calibration technician(s). In deference to costs, however, particularly where expertise is questionable, there are situations where this function is shared with an independent calibration laboratory.

2. An independent calibration laboratory   Intervals of calibration should be delegated to an independent laboratory when a history of objective calibration data is readily available.

3. The instrument manufacturer   An instrument manufacturer may provide instructions regarding the establishment of intervals of calibration. End users of the instrument are cautioned to establish calibration intervals that are based on the degree of usage.

Calibration records play an important role in the establishment of calibration intervals and interval adjustments. The justification of interval adjustments is predicated on data generated during previous calibrations. (See chapter 7 for an additional discussion of the effect of intervals of calibration.) When inspection records indicate that the inspection equipment requires frequent adjustments, the interval should be shortened and the pertinent data should be evaluated to determine their impact on out-of-tolerance conditions. Intervals may be lengthened if the results of previous calibrations provide positive indications that the accuracy of the equipment will not be adversely affected.

When no calibration history is generated for a particular measuring device, or when contractual requirements are silent regarding the application of a specific calibration interval for a given instrument, a track record must be established before deciding on a particular frequency of calibration. Under these conditions the following steps should be taken:

1. Calibrate the instrument prior to use for one week. During this period, if the history of calibration shows that no adjustments were required, proceed to the next step.

2. Calibrate the instrument weekly for four weeks. If a favorable history prevails during this period, proceed to the next step.

3. Calibrate the instrument once a month for six months. If after this period the records indicate no out-of-tolerance conditions, proceed to the next step.

4. Calibrate the instrument every six months for one year. If the calibration record shows that no out-of-tolerance conditions are in evidence, calibrate the instrument once a year.

5. When a significant out-of-tolerance condition (one that adversely affects an established calibration interval) becomes evident, revert to the previous steps 2, 3, or 4.

A recall system must be in place to assure that calibrations are performed within specified intervals. The establishment and maintenance of a recall location record is one method of assuring that calibration schedules are met (see Figures 2.4 and 2.5).

A temporary extension of calibration due dates may be authorized only when a favorable in-tolerance history is in evidence. Unless otherwise authorized by the customer, no shipments should be made to the customer until the pertinent measuring equipment has been found to be in-tolerance and calibration results are documented on the respective form furnished for this purpose.

CALIBRATION PROCEDURES

Written methods or procedures for calibrating M&TE and MS must be provided by the contractor to eliminate possible measurement inaccuracies due to differences in techniques, environmental

1. Nomenclature _____

2. Identification number _____   3. Instruction number _____

4. Calibration frequency _____

5. Item location _____

_____

_____

6. Date recalled	7. Calibration date	8. Assigned to	9. Date in service	10. Assigned by	11. Remarks
_____	_____	_____	_____	_____	_____
_____	_____	_____	_____	_____	_____
_____	_____	_____	_____	_____	_____
_____	_____	_____	_____	_____	_____
_____	_____	_____	_____	_____	_____
_____	_____	_____	_____	_____	_____
_____	_____	_____	_____	_____	_____
_____	_____	_____	_____	_____	_____
_____	_____	_____	_____	_____	_____

Figure 2.4   Measuring equipment recall/location record form.

conditions, or choices of higher-level standards. The preparation of a calibration procedure is based on functional and physical characteristics of the product design. A detailed review and analysis of drawings, specifications, and special contract quality requirements and related product characteristics and their special tolerances will lead to the identification of the M&TE that will be required to check the product. Figure 2.6 reflects the steps that lead to the application of required calibration procedures.

Block number	**Action**
1. Nomenclature	Enter the name of the instrument that is used within the calibration system.
2. Identification number	Enter the number that identifies the instrument.
3. Instruction number	Enter the instruction number shown in respective calibration procedure.
4. Calibration frequency	Enter the established calibration frequency.
5. Item location	Enter the calibration laboratory or inspection station where the measuring equipment is located as well as those locations at an independent laboratory or at the subcontractor's facility, when applicable.
6. Date recalled	Enter as appropriate.
7. Calibration date	Enter the date calibrated.
8. Assigned to	Enter the person and/or department that the equipment is assigned to.
9. Date in service	Enter as appropriate.
10. Assigned by	Enter the calibration technician's signature or initials.
11. Remarks	Enter as appropriate.

Figure 2.5   Instructions for preparing the measuring equipment recall/location record form.

There are three main sources of calibration procedures.

1. Procedures compiled by the product manufacturer

2. Published standards

3. Instrument manufacturer's recommended calibration procedures

When published standards or the instrument manufacturer's recommended procedures are not available to the product manufacturer, the manufacturer must prepare its own calibration procedures.

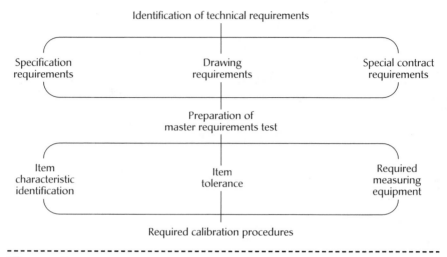

Identification of technical requirements

| Specification requirements | Drawing requirements | Special contract requirements |

Preparation of
master requirements test

| Item characteristic identification | Item tolerance | Required measuring equipment |

Required calibration procedures

Figure 2.6   Steps that lead to the application of required calibration procedures.

Product Manufacturer's Calibration Procedures

The product manufacturer's calibration procedures should address the factors shown in Figures 2.7 and 2.8 and must be upgraded when conditions warrant.

Published Standards

Published standards are available from participating members of the Government and Industry Data Exchange Program (GIDEP). Write to: Operations Center, Naval Weapons Station, Seal Beach, Corona, CA 91720.

GIDEP was established to conserve time, personnel, and money by eliminating redundant technical effort among government and industry design, research, development, engineering, and procurement programs.

Participation in the Metrology Data Interchange Program may be a contractual requirement. Organizations not having contracts that specify mandatory participation in the GIDEP program may participate on a voluntary basis by exchanging data applicable

1. Original/date _____   2. Revision/date _____

3. Instrument   4. Calibration
   nomenclature _____   procedure number _____

5. Instrument   6. Instrument   7. Instrument
   accuracy   range   discrimination

   _____   _____   _____

   _____   _____   _____

8. Measurement standards (MS)

   _____

   _____

9. Procedure

   _____

   _____

10. Name (preparer)/title/date _____

Figure 2.7   Calibration procedure form.

to the Metrology Data Bank and by providing annual reports of program benefits. Reports must be submitted at least once a year to continue participation in the program.

Instrument Manufacturer's Calibration Procedures

The instrument manufacturer's recommended calibration procedures are normally furnished with the purchased instrument. Occasionally these procedures may have to be ordered under separate cover. See Figure 2.9 for an example of an instrument manufacturer's calibration procedure.

ACCURACY OF MS AND M&TE

The selection of M&TE begins with knowing the product tolerances of items produced and the accuracy requirements of related M&TE. A decision to calibrate selected M&TE or MS in-house or

Block number	**Action**
1. Original/date	If the procedure was prepared first-hand, enter a check mark in the "original" block and the date that the procedure was prepared.
2. Revision/date	When a change is made to the calibration procedure, enter a check mark in the "revision" block and the date that the change was made.
3. Instrument nomenclature	Enter as appropriate.
4. Calibration procedure number	Enter a number that identifies the procedure.
5. Instrument accuracy	Enter the accuracy (discrimination) of the instrument that is to be calibrated.
6. Instrument range	Enter the range of the instrument that is to be calibrated. Example: If a zero to one inch micrometer is to be calibrated over its entire range, then enter "0–1."
	If the instrument is to be calibrated from zero to one-half inch, then enter "0–.500."
7. Instrument discrimination	Enter the smallest scale division of the instrument that is to be calibrated.
8. Measurement standards (MS)	a. Enter the name(s) of the MS that will be used to calibrate the instrument.
	b. Enter the accuracy of measurement standards.
	c. Remember to select only MS with a higher level of accuracy.
9. Procedure	Enter a step-by-step procedure that will satisfy calibration requirements for the instrument that is under calibration.
10. Name (preparer)/title/date	Enter as appropriate.

Figure 2.8   Instructions for preparing calibration procedures.

by an outside source such as an independent calibration laboratory is predicated on the volume of work, costs, technical capabilities, and the availability of facilities and equipment. For example, if the function of calibration is infrequent, then a study should be made to assess costs to perform these functions in-house as compared to using the services of an independent calibration laboratory.

Where there is a large volume of work that requires continuous repair and calibration of inspection, measuring, and test equipment,

BTG-1 Digital Gage Amplifier

1.	0-9, CLR,-	Used input information.
2.	MODE	Select probe A only, probe B only, or probe A and probe B together. The mode light will indicate which probes are selected.
3.	+/-	Changes the sign of the selected probe. Not valid when both probes are selected. When inputting information as in Mean, Gain, Offset, or Message, it allows entering a negative sign or dash.
4.	E/M	Select readings in inches or millimeters (English/metric).
5.	XMIT	Transmits information in display over RS-232 interface.
6.	HOLD	Freezes the current reading. To read new sizes, press the HOLD button again.
7.	PRINT	Prints the information in the display. Sizes are right-justified and messages are left-justified.
8.	ADV	Advances the printer.
9.	ENTER	Enters new information into the selected register.
10.	RANGE	Selects the range of the amplifier. The range lights will indicate which range is selected.
11.	ZERO	Allows zeroing readings to a zero master.
		a. Set up zero master.
		b. Press ZERO.
12.	MEAN	Allows setting a mean size.
		a. Set up zero master.
		b. Press ZERO.
		c. Press MEAN.
		d. Input Mean size using CLR, +/-, ., and 0-9.
		e. Press ENTER to store mean size.
		f. To clear a mean size, use the sequence MEAN, CLR, and ENTER.

Figure 2.9   A sample calibration procedure—keyboard functions.

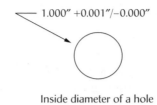

Inside diameter of a hole

Figure 2.10   Product tolerance in a unilateral direction.

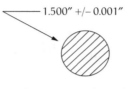

Outside diameter of a round bar stock

Figure 2.11   Product tolerance in a bilateral direction.

most companies use their own metrology specialists and their own calibration laboratory. In the case of both infrequent and continuous calibrations, however, many producers of products and services rely on both internal and external sources to calibrate and maintain the accuracy of their M&TE.

No two parts can be made exactly alike. This conclusion is shared with the design engineer, product manufacturer, and metrology manager in deference to interchangeability. To assure interchangeability of mating parts, the design engineer assigns a tolerance to product parameters. This tolerance allows for the variations inherent in the manufactured product, which are attributed to machine capabilities, people capabilities, and associated processes.

The calibration technician considers the product tolerance when selecting the best measuring equipment to verify product quality. Product tolerances may be referenced in a unilateral or bilateral direction (see Figures 2.10 and 2.11).

- Unilateral—A variation that is permitted in one direction from a specified dimension
- Bilateral—A variation that is permitted in two directions from a specified dimension

When instrument calibration is accomplished, the technician focuses on the discrimination of MS and related M&TE, as well as the accuracy ratio between the two.

When determining the adequacy of MS and M&TE, the technician monitors the potential measurement error, the area of uncertainty that exists on either side of every reading, and reduces the acceptable range of an acceptable reading by the prescribed tolerance of the measuring device (comparator). The technician allows for:

- The limitations inherent in the construction of M&TE
- The environmental conditions under which measurements are made
- The different ways the technician uses and reads measuring equipment

A high accuracy ratio between the comparator (MS or M&TE) and the item checked (M&TE or product) will provide a high degree of measurement confidence. Conversely, a low accuracy ratio will reflect a low degree of measurement confidence. Potential measurement error can be minimized with the proper selection of higher-level accuracy ratios between MS and M&TE (see Table 2.1).

With the exception of those conditions where state-of-the-art limitations preclude the use of accuracy ratios greater than 1:1, the selection of accuracy ratios between the comparator and the item that is being calibrated or inspected should be greater than 2:1 and preferably greater than 4:1. The examples shown in Figures 2.12, 2.13, 2.14, and 2.15, as well as Table 2.2, pertain to measurements that fall within an item's (instrument or product) tolerance range and are intended to show the impact that areas of uncertainty (or areas of acceptance) have on instrument adequacy.

A 1:1 accuracy ratio will reflect a 100 percent area of uncertainty; therefore all measurements that fall within an item's tolerance range will land in an area of uncertainty. Rejecting is normal when a measured value for those items falls outside of allowable tolerances.

Table 2.1   Impact of accuracy ratios.

Ratio	Area of acceptance	Area of uncertainty
1:1	0%	100%
2:1	50%	50%
4:1	75%	25%
10:1	90%	10%

Factors for determining accuracy ratios are:
R = Ratio
PT = Product tolerance
M&TAT = Measuring and test equipment accuracy tolerance
SAT = Secondary standard accuracy tolerance
PAT = Primary standard accuracy tolerance

Ratio selection:
a. Product manufacturer's prevailing (tightest) product tolerance = 0.005"
b. M&TAT = 0.001"
c. SAT = 0.0001"
d. PAT = 0.000004"

Ratio between M&TE tolerance and product tolerance:

$$R = \frac{PT}{M\&TAT} = \frac{0.005"}{0.001"}$$

$$= 5:1 \text{ (nominal)} = \text{ratio}$$

Ratio between secondary measurement standard and measuring and test equipment:

$$R = \frac{M\&TAT}{SAT} = \frac{0.001"}{0.0001"}$$

$$= 10:1 \text{ (nominal)} = \text{ratio}$$

Ratio between primary standard and secondary standard:

$$R = \frac{SAT}{PAT} = \frac{0.0001"}{0.000004"}$$

$$= 25:1 = \text{ratio}$$

It is important to note that a 1:1 accuracy ratio may or may not indicate that items calibrated under these conditions are in conformance with prescribed tolerances. A 1:1 accuracy ratio may not provide the required measurement confidence. In addition, it might lead to material review board (MRB) actions and unanticipated

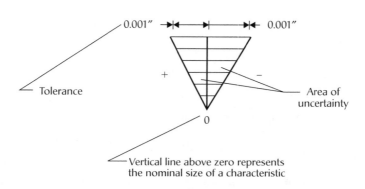

Item (instrument or product) tolerance = +/– 0.001″

$$\frac{\text{Tolerance (+/–)}}{\text{ratio}} = \frac{T}{R} = \frac{0.001''}{1} = 0.001 \quad \text{(Discrimination of comparator)}$$

Comparator

0.001″ ►◄ ► ►◄ 0.001″

+ –

Tolerance

Area of uncertainty

0

Vertical line above zero represents the nominal size of a characteristic

Figure 2.12   Example of a 1:1 accuracy ratio.

quality costs. An MRB consists of technical representatives employed by a product manufacturer whose primary responsibility is to determine or recommend the proper disposition of material referred to them.

A 4:1 accuracy ratio will reflect a 75 percent area of acceptance and a 25 percent area of uncertainty. A 10:1 accuracy ratio will reflect a 90 percent area of acceptance and a 10 percent area of uncertainty. The use of a ratio of 10:1 or greater will provide greater measurement confidence and will reduce potential measurement error.

When measurements fall within the area of acceptance, measurement confidence can be achieved. However, when measurements fall within an area of uncertainty, a decision to accept or reject a measurement might be questionable.

Measuring equipment with a high level of accuracy will greatly assist the technician in making the right decision to accept or reject measured readings.

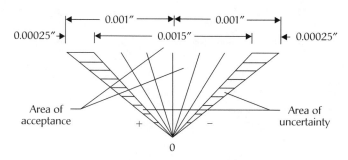

$$\text{Tolerance} = \frac{T}{R} = \frac{0.001''}{4} = 0.00025'' \begin{matrix} \text{(Discrimination} \\ \text{of comparator)} \end{matrix}$$

Comparator

0.00025" ⟶ | ← — 0.001" — ⟶ | ← — 0.001" — ⟶ | ← 0.00025"

| ← — — — 0.0015" — — — ⟶ |

Area of acceptance   Area of uncertainty

+   –

0

Comments:

a. The area of uncertainty is equal to the accuracy of the comparator.

b. When measurements fall in the area of uncertainty a determination must be made as to its impact in allowable tolerances.

For example: An allowable product tolerance for a one-inch diameter bar stock is +/– 0.001":

Actual measurement	= 1.001"
Area of uncertainty	= 0.00025"
Discrimination allowance	= ± 0.00025"
Therefore . . .	

The acceptable reading is considered to be between 1.00075" and 1.00125"

Conclusion is that the measurement can either be accepted at 1.00075" or rejected at 1.00125".

Figure 2.13 Example of a 4:1 accuracy ratio.

The technician must assure that accuracy ratios between the M&TE and the product tolerance and the MS and M&TE are adequate for the purpose intended. A ratio greater than 4:1 is acceptable. A ratio of 10:1 or greater, however, is recommended whenever possible. When measurements fall within an area of uncertainty, a decision must be made as to its impact on out-of-tolerance conditions.

Item (instrument or product) tolerance = 0.001"

$$\frac{\text{Tolerance } (+/-)}{\text{ratio}} = \frac{T}{R} = \frac{0.001"}{10} = 0.0001 \quad \begin{array}{l}\text{(Discrimination} \\ \text{of comparator)}\end{array}$$

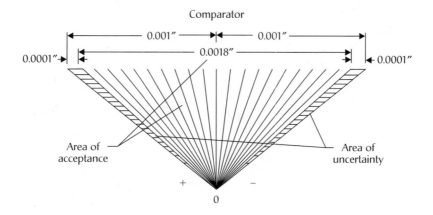

Comments:

a. The area of uncertainty is equal to the accuracy of the comparator.

b. When measurements fall in the area of uncertainty a determination must be made as to its impact on allowable tolerances.

For example: An allowable product tolerance for a one-inch diameter bar stock is +/– 0.001":

Actual measurement	= 1.001"
Area of uncertainty	= 0.0001"
Discrimination allowance	= ± 0.0001"
Therefore . . .	
The acceptable reading is considered to be between 1.0009" and 1.0011"	

Conclusion is that the measurement can either be accepted at 1.0009" or rejected at 1.0011".

Figure 2.14   Example of a 10:1 accuracy ratio.

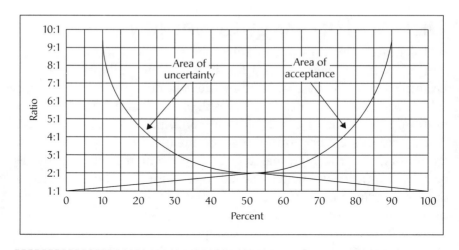

Figure 2.15   Representative curve for a product tolerance of 0.001″.

Table 2.2   Accuracy ratios between product tolerance and M&TE.

Ratio	Comparator discrimination	Area of uncertainty	Area of acceptance
1:1	0.001000″	100%	0%
2:1	0.000500″	50%	50%
3:1	0.000333″	33%	67%
4:1	0.000250″	25%	75%
5:1	0.000200″	20%	80%
6:1	0.000167″	16%	84%
7:1	0.000143″	14%	86%
8:1	0.000125″	13%	87%
9:1	0.000110″	11%	89%
10:1	0.000100″	10%	90%

OUT-OF-TOLERANCE CONDITIONS

In-tolerance as well as out-of-tolerance conditions are determined by the review of feedback data furnished by the calibration agency. Examples of forms that are used by the calibrating agency to record calibration data are found in Figures 2.16, 2.17, and 2.18. The calibration agency may be one of, or a combination of, the product manufacturer's calibration laboratory, an independent calibration laboratory, and the National Institute of Standards and Technology. Calibration data, which is used to assess in-tolerance as well as out-of-tolerance conditions, is provided by all of these organizations. Generally speaking, the product manufacturer generates calibration data associated with working inspection, measuring, and test equipment and some instruments that they classify as their MS, and an independent calibration laboratory will calibrate all other measurement standards and working instruments that a product manufacturer has elected to be calibrated by an outside calibration source.

Feedback data are reviewed and analyzed by the metrology manager or a designated representative at the time of calibration or shortly thereafter to determine

- The adequacy of established calibration intervals
- Whether there is a need to adjust calibration intervals
- Whether there is a need to modify established calibration procedures
- The adequacy of the calibration system and equipment reliability
- The identification and prevention of the use of any equipment found to be out-of-tolerance until the reported deficiency has been corrected

Out-of-tolerance conditions of MS and M&TE are placed into three general categories (conditions A, B, and C).

Calibration Record

Instrument ______________________________

Model ______________________ Location ______________________

I.d. no. ______________________ Accuracy ______________________

Procedure no. ______________________ Discrimination ______________________

Calibration freq. ______________________ Tamper-proof ☐ Yes ☐ No

Other ______________________________

____

Date calibrated	Due date	Calibration technician	Work performance									
			Characteristic identification									
			Measured value									

Figure 2.16 An example of a manufacturer's calibration record.

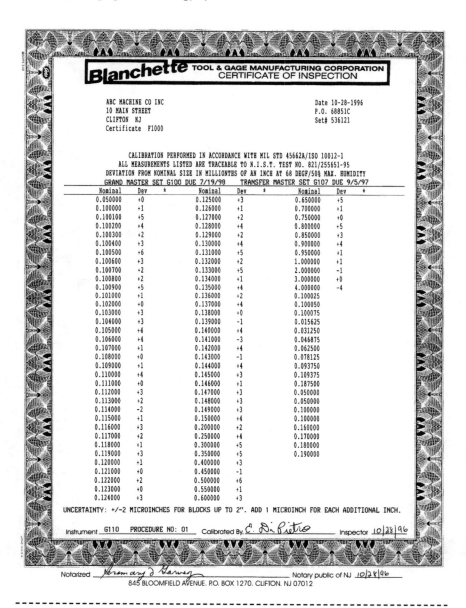

Figure 2.17   A sample certificate of inspection.

```
PROCEDURE NO. 01:  GAGE BLOCK INSPECTION  ALL GAGE BLOCKS ARE
CLEANED, DEBURRED AND CHECKED ON DUAL-JET GAGE BLOCK COMPARATORS
G109 OR G110.  AS PER DOCUMENT GGG-G-15C, MEASUREMENT IS TAKEN
AT SPECIFIED REFERENCE POINT, WITH DEVIATION FROM NOMINAL SIZE
SIZE GIVEN IN MILLIONTHS OF AN INCH

THE UNCERTAINTY OF MEASUREMENT FACTOR:  THE UNCERTAINTY OF
MEASUREMENT IS +/-2 MICROINCHES FOR BLOCKS UP TO AND INCLUDING
2 INCHES.  FOR BLOCKS EXCEEDING 2 INCHES, ADD 1 MICROINCH FOR
EACH ADDITIONAL INCH


N.I.S.T. TRACEABILITY NUMBERS:

_____     TEST NO. 821/255651-95.  GRAND MASTER SET G100
          SN 9.2572A+6.  CAL: 7-19-95  DUE: 7-19-98
_____     TRANSFER MASTER SET G107 CAL: 9-5-96  DUE: 9-5-97

_____     TEST NO. 821/253616-94.  WAFER MASTER SET G103/G104/G105
          SN EIG1686/ML05/JIK1687.  CAL: 8-29-94  DUE: 8-29-97

_____     TEST NO. 821/252163-93.  LONG RANGE MASTER SET G106
          SN 51280.16.  CAL: 1-20-94  DUE: 1-20-97

_____     TEST NO. 821/254855-95.  METRIC MASTER SET G101/G102
          SN 3876.1.  CAL: 11-28-95  DUE: 11-28-98
```

Figure 2.17   Continued.

Condition (ratio between MS and M&TE)	**Impact on accuracy requirements**
A (4:1 to 10:1 or greater)	The adequacy of MS and M&TE will be satisfactorily maintained. No action is required.
B (2:1 to less than 4:1)	When instrument accuracy deteriorates from condition A to condition B, investigate the applicable factors that contribute to this trend towards an out-of-tolerance condition.
C (ratio of less than 2:1)	When instrument accuracy deteriorates to condition C, it will have a major impact on the accuracy requirements of MS and M&TE. It is a significant condition that will require immediate corrective action. Investigate all of the factors that impact out-of-tolerance conditions. These factors are referenced later in this chapter.

Reprinted with permission from NIST
United States Department of Commerce
National Institute of Standards and Technology
Gaithersburg, Maryland 20899
Report of Calibration

Page 1 of 1

For: # OF BLOCKS

Serial no. _____

Submitted by: COMPANY NAME
ADDRESS

These gage blocks were compared with the standards of the United States. The comparison process employs electromechanical comparators and four gage blocks (two standards and two test blocks) in a least squares intercomparison schedule designed to eliminate the effects of thermal drift.

This process together with its statistical analysis constitutes a continuous measurement assurance program maintained at NIST to ensure that realistic uncertainty values are assigned to the length determinations. Details of the process are covered in NBSIR 80-2078, "The NBS Gage Block Calibration Process Using a Measurement Assurance Program," which is considered to be a part of this report.

The deviation in length from the nominal size at 20 degrees Celsius (68 degrees F) is given on the following pages along with total uncertainty for each gage block.

These blocks were compared with similar blocks from NIST Test No. _____ .

Measurements were made by _____ .

For the Director,
National Institute of Standards and Technology

Ralph C. Veale, Group Leader
Dimensional Metrology
Precision Engineering Division
Center for Manufacturing Engineering

Purchase Order No. _____

NIST Test No. _____

Date: _____

Figure 2.18   NIST report of calibration.

When an out-of-tolerance condition prevails, an investigation is required to determine

- The accuracy of MS used to calibrate M&TE
- The adequacy of M&TE used to check the product
- The adequacy of calibration intervals
- The quality of products accepted in-house, as well as the quality of products shipped to customers
- The adequacy of established calibration procedures

Attribute-type instruments (Go/Not Go gages) are considered significantly out-of-tolerance when their dimension sizes exceed the maximum and minimum material limits of a product's feature size. Significant out-of-tolerance conditions must be documented and brought to the attention of the responsible department supervisor(s) for appropriate action (see Figures 2.19 and 2.20).

CALIBRATION SOURCES

There are three main calibration sources. They are as follows:

1. A commercial facility, such as an independent calibration laboratory, with calibration equipment that is certified as being traceable to NIST
2. A contractor whose calibration is traceable directly to NIST or through an unbroken chain of properly conducted calibrations that are traceable to NIST
3. NIST, formerly known as the National Bureau of Standards

The following information is reprinted with permission from NIST:

> *On August 23, 1988, the President of the United States signed into law the Omnibus Trade and Competitiveness Act of 1988, including the Technology Competitiveness Act. The Act has created the National Institute of Standards and Technology (NIST) from the National Bureau of Standards (NBS).*

1. To _____

2. From _____

3. Report number _____   4. Date _____

5. Measuring device _____

6. Identification number _____   7. Calibration procedure number _____

8. Reply due date _____

9. Signature of requestor _____

10. Out-of-tolerance condition

11. Corrective action as to cause

12. Conclusion: Complaint is justified _____ not justified _____

13. Recommended corrective action

14. Investigator's signature _____

15. Title _____   16. Date _____

- -

Figure 2.19   Metrology deficiency report.

Block number	**Action**
1. To	Enter quality-control manager, metrology manager, or other (as applicable).
2. From	Enter name of the agency that performed the calibration.
3. Report number	Begin with number one for the first report, two for the second report, etc.
4. Date	Enter as appropriate.
5. Measuring device	Enter the instrument nomenclature.
6. Identification number	Enter as appropriate.
7. Calibration procedure number	Enter number shown in the respective calibration procedure.
8. Reply due date	Enter date established by the requestor.
9. Signature of requestor	Enter as appropriate.
10. Out-of-tolerance condition	Describe observed deficiency in detail. Attach supporting data when necessary.
11. Corrective action as to cause	Identify the cause of the deficiency that created the out-of-tolerance condition.
12. Conclusion	Determine if complaint is justified. Enter appropriate block.
13. Recommended corrective action	a. Recalibrate measuring device using high-action level accuracy standards. b. Upgrade calibration procedures. c. Reinspect the product with measuring equipment of known accuracy. d. Shorten calibration interval. e. Other as appropriate.
14., 15., and 16.	Enter as appropriate.

Figure 2.20   Instructions for preparing the metrology deficiency report.

Our new name reflects the increased responsibility assigned to our agency to support and enhance the technological competitiveness of U.S. industry, as well as our traditional function of providing measurements, calibrations, and quality assurance standards vital to U.S. industry.

The new law has provided a challenge as well as innovative mechanisms for NIST to aid industry. The institute is instructed to create a series of "Regional Centers for the Transfer of Manufacturing Technology" that will be affiliated with non-profit institutions or organizations. NIST is also to create a program to provide assistance and make federal technology available to state and local technology programs and technology extension services.

An "Advance Technology Program" will be established to encourage the commercialization of high technology products. NIST will also support a Department of Commerce Clearinghouse for State and Local Initiatives on Productivity, Technology, and Innovation, providing technical and analytical help to state and local officials making decisions on technology policy. Not all of these functions, however, are currently funded. Those services and research areas for which NBS has been known in the past will continue under NIST. In particular, our Standard Reference Materials, Standard Reference Data Programs, and calibration services will continue to serve the needs of American industry and science.

APPLICATION OF RECORDS

Recording the functions of quality is one of the best methods of providing objective quality evidence. Records are made of

- Work accomplished
- Compliance with work instructions
- Noncompliance with work instructions

Records that control and maintain the calibration system include the following:

Record	Purpose
Item identification	Tag or label instruments
Item history	Standard form (record of calibration)
Out-of-tolerance conditions	Standard form (triggers the need for the adjustment of calibration policies and/or procedures)
Calibration procedures	Step-by-step procedure to eliminate possible measurement inaccuracies

CALIBRATION STATUS

Calibration status is accomplished by the use of tags, labels, or codes. The selected method should, as a minimum, identify the date, month, and year that the instrument was calibrated as well as the calibration due date. Labels should be attached to the instrument. When it is impractical to attach a label to the instrument, it may be attached to the instrument's container.

Limited-use M&TE should be identified as such, as well as the range of the instrument. Obsolete and out-of-service instruments should be identified as such and stored apart from active equipment. Uncalibrated instruments should not be used.

CONTROL OF SUBCONTRACTOR CALIBRATION

The selection of capable subcontractors is the responsibility of both the purchasing and quality-control managers. Purchasing is responsible for procuring the supplies and services that are required for the support of a manufactured product. The purchasing manager coordinates the proposed subcontractor with the quality-control manager and alerts suppliers of pertinent calibration system requirements. The quality-control manager ensures that subcontracted supplies and services conform to purchase order requirements. He/she is also responsible for the review of suppliers' quality functions at intervals consistent with complexity and accuracy requirements of products and services offered by the supplier.

STORAGE AND HANDLING

M&TE should be placed in containers or wrapped in moisture-free barrier material and placed in suitable bins to assure that the equipment maintains the required level of accuracy. The equipment should also be carefully handled during movement and use.

MAINTENANCE OF POLICIES AND PROCEDURES

Quality-assurance personnel must have ready access to contract and product design changes. If policies and procedures are to be satisfactorily maintained, quality-assurance personnel must know of changes in technical requirements and other contract quality requirements to continually evaluate and determine the impact that those changes have on established policies and procedures. Timely and effective changes to established policies and procedures assure that maximum effort can be directed to the satisfactory maintenance of an established calibration system description.

Management must decide that employees who successfully apply a calibration system will be rewarded and recognized. When policies and procedures are written so that support documentation is in place and where an ongoing system for evaluation of a calibration system is maintained, the results will create

- A foundation for good quality
- A reinforcement of measurement confidence
- The enhancement of the quality expectations of the customer

Most of all, a well-maintained calibration system will have a positive impact on the quality of products and services offered to the customer.

Notes

1. ANSI/ASQC M1, 1987 American National Standard of Calibration Systems, clause 1, 1.
2. ISO/IEC Guide 25, 1990, General Requirements for the Competence of Calibration and Testing Laboratories, clauses 1.1 and 1.2, 1.
3. Ibid.
4. ANSI/NCSL Z540-1, 1994, American National Standards for Calibration, Calibration Laboratories and Measuring and Test Equipment—General Requirements, clauses 1.1, 1.2, and Clause 1.3, 1.
5. Ibid.
6. Ibid.
7. ISO 10012-1, 1992, Quality Assurance Requirements for Measuring Equipment—Part 1: Metrological Confirmation System for Measuring Equipment Clauses 1.1, 1.2, and 1.3, 1.
8. Ibid.
9. Ibid.
10. U.S. Department of Defense, General Services Administration, and National Aeronautics Space Administration, Federal Acquisition Regulation, 1995, Part 42, clause 42. 501.

CHAPTER 3

Metrology Audit

The supplier shall establish and maintain an effective documented system for the managing, confirmation and use of measuring equipment, including measurement standards, used to demonstrate compliance with specified requirements. This system shall be designed to ensure that all such measuring performs as intended. The system shall provide for the prevention of errors outside the specified limits of permissible error, by prompt detection of deficiencies and by timely action for their correction. The confirmation system shall take full account of all relevant data, including that available from any statistical process control system operated by or for the Supplier.[1]

Auditors

Metrology audits are predicated on need. An audit may be performed on only one, a few, or all of the applicable elements of an adopted calibration system standard. Internal audits are conducted to verify that documented policy, procedures, and processes are being followed. The auditor also supports top management in its attempt to improve established procedures and processes.

The functions of a metrology audit should be performed by certified or experienced quality-assurance specialists who do not have specific responsibilities in the area audited. The auditors should be familiar with the appropriate portions of a documented quality plan and associated procedures and processes. Audit responsibilities may be delegated by the director of quality assurance to only one member of his/her staff or to an independent consultant. If the audit is complex in nature, however, this function may be delegated to a team of specialists consisting of the director of quality assurance, quality engineer, metrology manager, and calibration technician.

External metrology audits are conducted in situations where a prime contractor decides to delegate some or all of the metrology functions to an independent calibration laboratory.

Review of Policies and Procedures

A calibration system audit begins with the review of established policies and procedures followed by the verification of those policies and procedures at the respective calibration site(s) and inspection station(s). If documented policies and procedures are not available at the time of the scheduled audit, or if they are considered inadequate, a report of these findings should be brought to the attention of the responsible department supervisor. The audit team must then terminate the calibration audit but continue to perform an audit of operations (when this action is determined by the team leader to be in the best interest of the quality-assurance process) or reschedule the audit sometime after the required documentation is in place and put into operation. The timely review of documented policies and procedures is a "table setting" operation to assure that all requirements of a calibration system have been addressed by a supplier and are included in a master quality plan.

DEGREE OF APPLICATION

After the system description is found to be acceptable and in place, a determination will then be made as to the degree of audit application. The following elements form the basis for preparing audit checklists. They are followed by a list of factors associated with a metrology system. It is important to note that the factors listed under each of these elements are provided for information purposes only. They are generic in nature, should not be stereotyped, and should be used as a reference and only if the factors apply to a specific contract quality requirement, a quality plan, or associated policy, procedure, or process.

1. Intervals of calibration
2. Out-of-tolerance conditions
3. Calibration system requirements
4. Adequacy of measurement standards
5. Environmental controls
6. Calibration procedures
7. Calibration sources
8. Application of records
9. Calibration status
10. Control of subcontractor calibration
11. Purchaser-supplied M&TE
12. Storage and handling
13. Inventory control
14. Capabilities
15. Sealing for integrity
16. Traceability of documentation

AUDIT CHECKLIST

An audit checklist should be prepared in advance of the actual audit for each element of the system that is to be audited, and it should address the following:

1. Name of element evaluated   An element of a calibration system is selected from documentation referenced in an established quality plan. The selected element (one or more) is predicated on the needs, expectations, and objectives of a proposed audit.

2. Characteristics evaluated   Selected metrology audit characteristics may be related to a system (policy and procedures) or to an item (instrument or product).

3. Pertinent section and paragraph of the documented system scheduled to be evaluated   Appropriate sections and paragraphs are selected from established policy, procedures, processes, and work instructions.

4. Adequacy or inadequacy of the system description   The adequacy or inadequacy of a metrology system begins with the review of documented policy and procedures during an off-site "desk audit," which is followed by an on-site audit verification of predetermined elements and associated factors.

5. Adequacy or inadequacy of systems application   The adequacy/inadequacy of a metrology system starts with the assessment of unbiased characteristics identified during the desk audit. These characteristics are then assessed at preselected inspection and calibration stations. The results of these assessments form the basis for verifying the adequacy/inadequacy of the system.

Checklists of the major elements that comprise the system description are shown in Figures 3.1 through 3.16.*

----

*The checklists shown in Figures 3.1 through 3.16 shall be implemented as required, as well as other element factors that will impact contract quality requirements.

Requirement	References	Documentation		application	
		Sat.	Unsat.	Sat.	Unsat.
Element: Intervals of calibration, section _____					
Characteristics:					
Basis for establishing intervals of calibration	Para. no. ____	*	*	*	*
Adequacy of recall system	Para. no. ____	*	*	*	*
Adequacy of historical records	Para. no. ____	*	*	*	*
Calibration due date	Para. no. ____	*	*	*	*
Prompt release of measuring equipment	Para. no. ____	*	*	*	*
Overdue notices	Para. no. ____	*	*	*	*
Basis for adjusting calibration intervals	Para. no. ____	*	*	*	*

Figure 3.1   Calibration system checklist.

Requirement	References	Sat.	Unsat.	Sat.	Unsat.
Element: Out-of-tolerance conditions, section ____					
Characteristics:					
Definition of significant out-of-tolerance condition	Para. no. ____	*	*	*	*
Adequacy of standards	Para. no. ____	*	*	*	*
Adjustment and use prevention of equipment that does not perform satisfactorily	Para. no. ____	*	*	*	*
Adjustment of calibration levels	Para. no. ____	*	*	*	*
Notification of reporting channels of out-of-tolerance conditions	Para. no. ____	*	*	*	*

*Enter check mark if documentation and related application process is considered

Figure 3.2   Calibration system checklist.

Requirement	References	Documentation application			
		Sat.	Unsat.	Sat.	Unsat.
Element: Calibration system requirement, section ____					
Evaluation factors:					
Documentation of specified calibration/confirmation model	Para. no. ____	*	*	*	*
Complete documentation of prescribed calibration system	Para. no. ____	*	*	*	*
Management's commitment to the objective of calibration systems management	Para. no. ____	*	*	*	*
Management review and approval of written policy and procedures	Para. no. ____	*	*	*	*
Procedures for the control of written policy and procedures	Para. no. ____	*	*	*	*
Documentation of organizational chart and responsibilities	Para. no. ____	*	*	*	*
Job description of key technical and management personnel	Para. no. ____	*	*	*	*
Documented traceability of:					
a. Product characteristic to the appropriate contract	Para. no. ____	*	*	*	*
b. Product characteristic to the associated M&TE	Para. no. ____	*	*	*	*
c. M&TE to the appropriate measurement standard (MS)	Para. no. ____	*	*	*	*
d. MS to an international or domestic standard	Para. no. ____	*	*	*	*
Provisions for the preparation or upgrading of quality plans associated with new product designs	Para. no. ____	*	*	*	*

Figure 3.3   Calibration system checklist.

Element: Adequacy of
measurement standards, section ____

Evaluation factors:

Accuracy	Para. no. ____	*	*	*	*
Stability	Para. no. ____	*	*	*	*
Range	Para. no. ____	*	*	*	*
Resolution	Para. no. ____	*	*	*	*

Figure 3.4   Calibration system checklist.

Element:
Environment, section ____

Evaluation factors:

Conditions that affect the accuracy and stability of M&TE and MS	Para. no. ____	*	*	*	*
Compensations and/or corrections are applied where defined environmental conditions are not met	Para. no. ____	*	*	*	*

Figure 3.5   Calibration system checklist.

Element: Calibration
procedures, section ____

Evaluation factors:

Method of calibration	Para. no. ____	*	*	*	*
Name of measuring instrument to be calibrated	Para. no. ____	*	*	*	*
Calibration procedure original, revision, or deletion date	Para. no. ____	*	*	*	*
Identification number of calibration procedure	Para. no. ____	*	*	*	*
Higher-level MS (primary and/or secondary)	Para. no. ____	*	*	*	*
Accuracy of MS	Para. no. ____	*	*	*	*
Environmental conditions	Para. no. ____	*	*	*	*
Application of correction factors (where appropriate)	Para. no. ____	*	*	*	*
Data (attribute and/ or variable)	Para. no. ____	*	*	*	*

Figure 3.6   Calibration system checklist.

Sources of calibration procedure:

a. Standard procedures	Para. no. _____	*	*	*	*
b. Instrument manufacturer's recommended procedures	Para. no. _____	*	*	*	*
c. Product manufacturer's established procedures	Para. no. _____	*	*	*	*
Verification of inspection, measuring, and test procedures	Para. no. _____	*	*	*	*
Documented procedures which assure that calibrated instruments are suitably identified	Para. no. _____	*	*	*	*
Procedures for handling instruments	Para. no. _____	*	*	*	*
Procedure for the identification of M&TE and MS	Para. no. _____	*	*	*	*
Procedures for feedback data associated with out-of-tolerance M&TE and MS	Para. no. _____	*	*	*	*
Procedures for dealing with internal and external complaints	Para. no. _____	*	*	*	*
Procedures for protecting proprietary rights	Para. no. _____	*	*	*	*
Documented procedures for the performance of internal and external audits	Para. no. _____	*	*	*	*
Review and analysis of customer's requirements	Para. no. _____	*	*	*	*
Availability of complete technical data package	Para. no. _____	*	*	*	*
Financial, production, purchasing, and quality-assurance resources	Para. no. _____	*	*	*	*
Audit of established policy and procedures	Para. no. _____	*	*	*	*

Figure 3.6   Continued.

Element: Calibration
sources, section _____

Evaluation factors:

National Institute of Standards and Technology	Para. no. _____	*	*	*	*
Independent calibration laboratory	Para. no. _____	*	*	*	*
Instrument manufacturer	Para. no. _____	*	*	*	*
Product manufacturer	Para. no. _____	*	*	*	*
Derived from accepted values of natural physical constants	Para. no. _____	*	*	*	*

Supporting data:

a. Certification	Para. no. _____	*	*	*	*
b. Report numbers	Para. no. _____	*	*	*	*
c. Certificate number	Para. no. _____	*	*	*	*
d. Data sheets	Para. no. _____	*	*	*	*
e. Accuracy of MS	Para. no. _____	*	*	*	*
f. Environmental conditions	Para. no. _____	*	*	*	*
g. Compliance with an appropriate system standard	Para. no. _____	*	*	*	*
h. International standard	Para. no. _____	*	*	*	*

Figure 3.7   Calibration system checklist.

Element: Application of
records, section _____

Evaluation factors:

Instrument identification	Para. no. _____	*	*	*	*
Calibration schedules	Para. no. _____	*	*	*	*
Current calibration interval	Para. no. _____	*	*	*	*
Date of last calibration	Para. no. _____	*	*	*	*
Calibration source	Para. no. _____	*	*	*	*
Calibration procedure	Para. no. _____	*	*	*	*
Corrective action taken	Para. no. _____	*	*	*	*
Indication of operational failure	Para. no. _____	*	*	*	*
Calibration certificate of report number	Para. no. _____	*	*	*	*

Figure 3.8   Calibration system checklist.

Element: Calibration
status, section _____

Evaluation factors:

Identified throughout the production and installation process	Para. no. _____	*	*	*	*
Identification or limited-use M&TE	Para. no. _____	*	*	*	*
Tamper-proof seals affixed where appropriate	Para. no. _____	*	*	*	*

Figure 3.9   Calibration system checklist.

Element: Control of subcontractor
calibration, section _____

Evaluation factors:

Appropriate requirements imposed on subcontractor	Para. no. _____	*	*	*	*
Audit of subcontractors	Para. no. _____	*	*	*	*

Figure 3.10   Calibration system checklist.

Element: Purchaser-
supplied M&TE, section _____

Evaluation factors:

Controlled in accordance with prescribed contract or purchase order requirements	Para. no. _____	*	*	*	*

Figure 3.11   Calibration system checklist.

Element:
Storage and handling, section _____

Evaluation factors:

M&TE and MS are
protected during:

a. Storage	Para. no. _____	*	*	*	*
b. Handling	Para. no. _____	*	*	*	*
c. Transportation	Para. no. _____	*	*	*	*

Method of packaging
during storage as well
as while in use   Para. no. _____   *   *   *   *

Figure 3.12 Calibration system checklist.

Element: Inventory
control, section _____

Evaluation factors:

Date of inventory	Para. no. _____	*	*	*	*
Name of instrument	Para. no. _____	*	*	*	*
Accuracy of M&TE	Para. no. _____	*	*	*	*
Accuracy of MS (certified)	Para. no. _____	*	*	*	*
Active/inactive instruments	Para. no. _____	*	*	*	*

Figure 3.13   Calibration system checklist

Element: Capabilities,
section _____

Evaluation factors:

Internal	Para. no. _____	*	*	*	*
External	Para. no. _____	*	*	*	*

Figure 3.14   Calibration system checklist.

Element: Sealing for
integrity, section ____

Evaluation factors:

Procedure for safeguarding
M&TE and MS:

a. Method   Para. no. ____   *   *   *   *

Figure 3.15   Calibration system checklist.

Element: Traceability
documentation and
verification, section ____

Evaluation factors:

International standards   Para. no. ____   *   *   *   *

National standards   Para. no. ____   *   *   *   *

Certificates   Para. no. ____   *   *   *   *

Reports   Para. no. ____   *   *   *   *

Data sheets   Para. no. ____   *   *   *   *

*Enter check mark where documentation and
related application process is considered.

Figure 3.16   Calibration system checklist.

REPORT

A report of findings regarding the ongoing capabilities of a supplier's operations or the capabilities of a subcontractor's operation should be prepared shortly after completion of the audit and should include the information specified in Figure 3.17 and completed as instructed in Figure 3.18.

When an exit interview is conducted between members of the audit team and supplier management personnel, a copy of the minutes of the meeting should be attached to the audit summary report (see Figure 3.17). The minutes of the exit interview (or conference) are usually taken by a member of the audit team. The minutes should indicate whether observed conditions were found to be conforming or nonconforming with established policies and procedures.

1. Name of facility _____

2. Location _____

3. Calibration system requirement _____

4. Inspection system/quality program requirements

5. Special contract quality requirements

6. Organizational structure

7. Names of key quality-assurance personnel

8. Total number of employees _____

9. Size of facility (square feet) _____

10. Customer references (optional) _____

11. Recommendation: Approve _____ Disapprove _____

12. Provide full substantiation of recommendation

13. Surveyed by _____   14. Date _____

15. Approved by _____   16. Date _____

Figure 3.17   Calibration system audit summary report (external).

Block number	**Action**
1. Name of facility	Enter the name of the facility audited.
2. Location	Enter the address of the facility audited.
3. Calibration system requirement	Enter the title of the calibration system that is referenced in the purchase agreement between the customer and supplier.
4. Inspection system/quality program requirements	This requirement pertains to prime contractors and subcontractors involved in the production of an end item for which a calibration system is a specified requirement of an inspection system or quality program.
5. Special contract quality requirements	Enter as applicable.
6. Organizational structure	Obtain a copy of the company's organizational flow chart, which covers the duties of the metrology department. Attach a copy of the flow chart to the audit report. State in this block that the flow chart is attached to the report.
7. Names of key quality-assurance personnel	Enter as appropriate.
8. Total number of employees	Enter number of employees (all departments).
9. Size of facility	Enter total of square feet under roof.
10. Customer references (optional)	Enter the name(s) of facilities that have production experience with the audited facility regarding the application of the same or similar calibration system requirements.
11. Recommendation	Check approve or disapprove, as applicable.
12. Provide full substantiation of recommendation	a. Substantiate conclusions and recommendations with factual data. b. When applicable, identify procedures and documentation as well as instruments that are not in compliance with established calibration system requirements. c. Attach a copy of the audit checklist to the report.
13. Surveyed by	a. Enter the name of the person who conducted the audit. b. If the audit is conducted by a team, enter the team leader's name and attach a list of team participants to the report.
14. Date	Enter as appropriate.
15. Approved by	Enter the name of the quality-control manager or a designated representative.
16. Date	Enter as appropriate.

Figure 3.18 Instructions for completing audit summary report (external).

1. Department audited

2. Person(s) contacted

3. Verification stations audited

4. System elements audited

5. Calibration characteristics checked

6. Conclusions/recommendations: Conforming _____ Nonconforming _____

7. Audited by _____   8. Title _____

9. Date _____

10. Approved by _____   11. Title _____

12. Date _____

Figure 3.19   Calibration system audit summary report (internal).

When no deficiencies are observed, the responsible management personnel should be advised of conforming performances and so noted in the minutes. If nonconforming conditions are in evidence, the observations should be clearly stated in the report. In addition, the report should clearly explain how each deficiency relates to a specific

- Contract quality requirement
- Calibration system description
- Calibration procedure
- Work instruction

When corrective action is requested by the auditing team, action items and those responsible for them should be clearly identified. When multiple deficiencies are encountered, a milestone chart should be implemented to monitor the corrective action process.

Block number	**Action**
1. Department audited	Enter as appropriate.
2. Person(s) contacted	Enter name of department supervisor.
3. Verification stations audited	Enter inspection station(s) and/or calibration station(s) where the audit was conducted.
4. System elements audited	Enter elements of the calibration system audited. Attach a copy of the respective audit checklist to the report.
5. Calibration characteristics checked	Enter list of instrument calibration characteristics that were observed to support the audit report.
6. Conclusions/recommendations	Substantiate conclusions and recommendations with factual data. Identify processes and documentation that are not in compliance with established calibration system requirements.
7. Audited by	Enter name(s) of person(s) that conducted the audit.
8. Title	Enter as appropriate.
9. Date	Enter as appropriate.
10. Approved by	Enter name of responsible management supervisor.
11. Title	Enter as appropriate.
12. Date	Enter as appropriate.

Figure 3.20   Instructions for preparing audit summary report (internal).

At a minimum, the chart should address

- Distribution of audit findings (within 10 working days)
- List of nonconformances
- Anticipated date of correction of each deficiency
- Anticipated date of corrective report (within 30 days)

If more than 30 days are required to accomplish satisfactory corrective action, arrangements should be made for mutually agreed-upon progress reports. The progress report should be shown on a milestone schedule and supported with a cover letter.

A supplier's internal report of findings should address the information specified in the calibration audit summary report (see Figure 3.19) and completed as instructed in Figure 3.20.

An audit is analogous to the "can't see the forest for the trees" syndrome because an owner of a process will not always see all of the areas that may provide opportunities for improvements. Because of an auditor's specialized training and singular focus, however, he/she is better equipped to make recommendations for improvements in established policy, processes, and procedures to management personnel where appropriate.

When conducting a metrology audit caution must be taken to select only those elements of a calibration system and their related factors that can be traceable to active documents. These active documents include policy, procedures, and processes. Where applicable, selected characteristics should be traceable to a specific contract or purchase order. This method of conducting an audit will provide both internal and external customers with assurance that the supplier of metrology services is (or is not) complying with the written quality plan and that associated policy, procedures, and processes are (or are not) accomplishing their intended purpose for controlling specified quality requirements.

Notes

1. ISO 10012-1, 1992, Quality Assurance Requirements for Measuring Equipment—Part 1: Metrological Confirmation System for Measuring Equipment, clause 4.3, 4.

CHAPTER 4

Case Study 1–Supplier with Unknown Calibration System Capabilities

The customer's primary concern is for the causes of inadequate production processes to be immediately identified and corrected, so as to assure that product quality is maintained and delivery schedules are met.

The supplier is concerned about the problems in production processes that lead to added quality costs and delays in delivery schedules. The supplier also fears possible loss of repeat business caused by inadvertently delivering nonconforming products to the customer.

This case study may be used in two ways. Obviously, it demonstrates how proper preparation makes the product's sale, production, and delivery easier for both the supplier and customer. But perhaps, more importantly, the case study assists the prime contractor to examine the quality and calibration systems of its suppliers. The case study encourages the use of the audit to improve capability in cases where initial review may find elements of compliance inadequate.

This case study is also intended to show the negative impact that errors of omission described in chapter 1 have on a proposed supplier when the supplier cannot provide satisfactory evidence of its quality-assurance capabilities during the customer's preaward survey. "Preaward survey" means *an evaluation by a surveying activity of a prospective contractor's (supplier) capability to perform a proposed contract.*[1] It is conducted by a team consisting of financial, production, and quality-assurance representatives. Occasionally a safety specialist is added to the team when conditions warrant; however, this text is focused only on the functions of quality-assurance personnel.*

The preaward survey supports the belief that requesting the lowest bidder is only the first step in the solicitation process. The customer must also assure that potential suppliers are responsible and have the capability to meet the technical requirements of a solicitation (proposed contract). The customer places heavy reliance on the technology and capabilities of its suppliers. This reliance must be established or maintained prior to issuing a contract award where a potential supplier's capability is unknown. The reliance is maintained on an ongoing basis where a supplier's capabilities provide assurance that products and services offered are in accordance with a prescribed requirement.

There are several factors that a supplier must address when establishing evidence of its own capabilities. In addition to having financial and production resources or the ability to obtain them within the time constraints required by the customer, a supplier must (a) be able to comply with a specified performance and delivery schedule, (b) have a satisfactory performance regarding the production of identical or similar items solicited, (c) have required

----

*Most preaward surveys that are performed at a proposed supplier's facility pertain to the inspection system or a quality program's capabilities; however, this book is focused on the calibration system that forms a part of a specified inspection system or quality program.

measuring equipment of known accuracy, and (d) have the ability to obtain additional resources that may be required.

Customers try to preclude the possibility of awarding a contract to an apparent low bidder with unknown capabilities. Experienced purchasers generally add a provision to their solicitation that will permit a quality-assurance representative to conduct an in-plant audit to assure that the proposed supplier has an acceptable calibration system in place. The customer wants to be assured that the system is current and, where necessary, will be upgraded appropriately.

The fact that all of the required calibration documentation is not readily available to an auditor does not necessarily mean that work will not be awarded. The customer may examine all of the facts associated with the solicited statement of work. This is particularly apparent when a low bidder indicates that its company has extensive experience in the production of similar items. An in-depth analysis of existing documentation and discussions between the auditor and key supplier personnel will enhance the decision process that will ultimately be in the best interest of both supplier and low bidder. For example, a decision to recommend an affirmative or negative contract award without addressing all of the elements of the system and associated factors that impact a specified calibration system can lead to errors of omission. When the results of an audit indicate that a supplier has a satisfactory performance record and that acceptable policies and procedures are in place, it reduces the risk of producing a product with measuring instruments of questionable accuracy.

When evidence of a supplier's quality-assurance capabilities is not available at the time of the survey but when the auditor(s) determine that the supplier understands the proposed contract quality requirements, the supplier may offset negative factors and support its case with satisfactory planning. Under this condition, the survey team may consider the supplier's request for the contract award to the purchaser after satisfactory documented planning is made available.

If the survey team decides that a proposed supplier's planning is inadequate, then the team will have no other recourse but to submit a "No Award" recommendation to the purchaser.

The following factors support an effective plan for remediation:

1. *Identification of proposed contract quality requirements on a milestone chart or other acceptable method* Milestone planning is a process by which the efforts of quality-assurance personnel responsible for the implementation and maintenance of metrology requirements shall be conducted and integrated through a comprehensive quality plan. The primary purpose of milestone planning is to ensure and make evident that specified requirements of a metrology system meet both internal and external customers' needs and expectations in a timely manner.

2. *Making arrangements for the acquisition of the required inspection, measuring, and test equipment (M&TE) and measurement standards (MS)* The proposed supplier seeks those companies that have the required elements in place. The supplier must act with the same diligence that its customer employs.

3. *Determining the requirements as well as the availability of additional quality-assurance personnel* The acquisition of additional quality-assurance personnel may offset deficiencies, if cost efficient. Where specified skills are not available within the organization, they can be acquired from an independent calibration laboratory or from a qualified consultant.

4. *Identifying the availability and capability of capable outside calibration sources* The availability of outside calibration sources is normally identified from a companies list of approved calibration sources or from an ANSI/ISO/ASQC Q9000 list of certified and registered companies. Where it is determined that a proposed source of calibration is not referenced on any of these lists, however, it is incumbent upon the prime contractor to verify a proposed supplier's calibration capability before a purchase order is awarded to a subcontractor.

When actions regarding these four steps are addressed, the supplier who initially did not have a calibration system in place at the time of the preaward survey may compete for business and produce effectively. A supplier that is able to plan and act on remediate often proves to be an acceptable supplier of products and services.

From: Contract administrator

To: Quality-control manager

1. Technical data requirements:
    a. Part name; valve, hydraulic service
    b. Quantity: 100 each
    c. Assembly drawing number: XXX456-1X
    d. Inspection system requirements: MIL-I-45208A
    e. Calibration system requirements: MIL-STD 45662A

2. Performance requirements:
    a. No leaks will be permitted when the valve is subjected to a hydrostatic test pressure of 6000 psig with the valve in the open position.
    b. Any weeping, porosity, or permanent deformation shall be cause for rejection.

3. Product inspection site: point of production

4. Product acceptance point: point of production

5. F.O.B. point: destination

6. Attachments:
    a. Assembly drawing
    b. Component drawings

7. Customer: U.S. Government

8. Delivery schedule: 180 days (by 7/3/9X)

Figure 4.1   Abstract of solicitation requirements.

With a minimum amount of guidance and an opportunity to prove its capability, it will not only produce acceptable products but also support methods for controlling product quality.

When a proposed supplier reflects a clear understanding of the technical requirements of a solicitation, it eliminates the impression that its capabilities are inadequate (see Figures 4.1 and 4.2).

In this case study, the proposed contractor's policies and procedures and calibration documentation are insufficient to adequately determine its quality-assurance capabilities. Under the present condition, the calibration system does not cover the quality-assurance requirements of the solicitation.

The conditions previously mentioned were brought to the attention of the company's president and quality-control manager

Contractor: John Doe Corporation

Purpose: To determine subject contractor's capabilities regarding the application of
            MIL-STD-45662A calibration system requirements

Persons contacted:
   a. President
   b. Quality-control manager

Supplier's quality-assurance structure:

Position	Years of experience
Quality-control manager	18
Inspection supervisor	12
Calibration technician	9
Four product inspectors	Average 11 years

Types of products produced:
   Mechanical components and assemblies with product tolerances of from
   0.001–0.0001 inch.

Size of plant:
   a. Size of tract: 4000 square feet
   b. Area under roof: 3200 square feet
   c. Number of buildings: one
   d. Kind of structure: cinder block

Calibration facilities and equipment:
   a. Calibration room: 225 square feet
   b. Measurement standards: precision gage blocks
   c. M&TE: a sufficient amount to satisfy solicitation requirements

Observations:
   a. The proposed contractor maintains an informal calibration system and relies on verbal
      orders to accomplish many of the functions of the calibration process.
   b. The calibration technician is wholly responsible for performing instrument calibration.
      No written instructions are furnished for this purpose.
   c. Calibration documentation is limited to the application of calibration labels to the
      respective instruments.

Figure 4.2   Preaward survey report.

at a meeting held in the company's conference room. The president recognized the shortcomings and stated that this was the company's first experience with the application of calibration systems management and that he was made aware by the quality-control manager of what was needed to upgrade the required policies and procedures. He also advised that additional personnel and outside assistance would be acquired to prepare and/or upgrade

Topic	Scheduled completion dates		
1. Planning	*** 1/14/9X		
2. Personnel	*** 1/14/9X		
3. Inspection equipment	*** 1/14/9X		
4. Calibration sources	*** 1/14/9X		
5 Written calibration description	· · · · · ·· · · · · · · · · · · · · · ·· · · · · · · · · · ·· · · · · · · · · · · ·· · · ·		
a. Responsibilities	***	2/7/9X	
b. System maintenance	***	2/7/9X	
c. Calibration intervals	***	2/7/9X	
d. Traceability of measurement standards	***	2/7/9X	
e. Environmental controls	***	2/7/9X	
f. Calibration status	***		2/14/9X
g. Objective evidence			2/14/9X
h. Calibration audits			3/14/9X

Legend: *** = Ongoing process

Figure 4.3   Milestone chart calibration system requirements.

pertinent policies, procedures, and documentation within the time constraints of the solicitation. The president's comments were supported with a schedule of anticipated completion dates (see Figure 4.3). However, a decision regarding the proposed supplier's ability to meet the solicitation requirements was held in abeyance pending the examination of three instruments that were previously calibrated by the proposed supplier. This was accomplished by checking three instruments—a 0–2000 psig pressure gage, a one-inch micrometer, and a twelve-inch vernier caliper— as well as the adequacy of conditions within the calibration area.

CALIBRATION AREA

- The calibration area was found to be clean and free from extraneous items.
- The room temperature in the calibration area was stabilized at 68° F.
- Instruments were properly protected in containers and when not in use they are stored safely in cabinets.

- Surface plates where calibrations are made were found to be calibrated by an independent calibration laboratory and they were free from nicks, cracks, and extraneous items.
- Reference standards were also calibrated by an independent laboratory.
- Calibrations provided by an independent laboratory were supported with a certified report, which included quality data showing the results of measurements made, applicable calibration system adopted, and satisfactory evidence of traceability of its laboratory standards by an unbroken chain of calibration events to the National Institute of Standards and Technology (NIST), and was signed by an official of the organization responsible for providing the calibration service.

INSTRUMENT ASSESSMENTS
Pressure Gage
Supporting Information
- Identification number: PR-101
- Instrument accuracy: +/− 10 psig
- Instrument range: 0–2000 psig
- Usage: Up to 600 psig
- Company's reference standard consisted of a pressure gage with a 10:1 accuracy ratio.

Note: The company's reference (transfer) standard, which is used to calibrate its working pressure gage, was calibrated by an independent laboratory with the use of a deadweight tester having an accuracy of +/− 0.1 percent of output pressure whose accuracy is traceable to NIST.

Assessment
The working pressure gage and the reference standard were examined for physical damage prior to integrating them into the test standard. It was noted that with no pressure on the gage scheduled for verification, the indicating needle was not located directly over

the zero reading. This was immediately rectified by accessing an adjustment device located on the gage and adjusting the indicator directly over the zero.

It is important to note that, although the inspection pressure gage in question was capable of testing pressures up to 2000 psig, the maximum pressure test required by the product specification was 600 psig. Therefore, this fact was taken into consideration when selecting pressure values for verification of the adequacy of instruments examined as well as associated policy and procedures.

Characteristics examined	Supplier's observations	Auditor findings*
100 psig	105 psig	105 psig
200 psig	205 psig	205 psig
300 psig	305 psig	305 psig
400 psig	405 psig	405 psig
500 psig	505 psig	505 psig
600 psig	605 psig	605 psig

One-inch Micrometer

Supporting Information

- Identification number: MI-201
- Discrimination: 0.0001 inch
- Instrument Accuracy: +/− 0.0001 inch
- Instrument range: 0–1.000 inch
- Usage: Full range
- Company standards consist of (a) a set of precision gage blocks, style 1 (rectangle) consisting of 81 blocks with a tolerance of +8 and −5 microinches, and (b) a precision measuring ball, size 0.12500 inch with an accuracy of 0.0002 inch.

----

*Compensating correction factor of 5 psig added to the calibration status tag to accommodate departures from the nominal values shown under the first column. This status tag is conspicuously attached to the working gage and in full view of the calibration and testing technician.

Assessment

Assessments were made on the calibration characteristics that were previously checked by the company's metrology specialist using precision gage blocks values of 0.100-, 0.200-, 0.450-, 0.750-, and 0.950-inch standards. The instrument was examined for physical and mechanical damage and subsequently checked in an area that was dust and particle free and on instrument measuring surfaces that were cleaned with a dust-free cloth. Verification of the supplier's observation was accomplished subsequent to verifying the flatness of the micrometer anvil.

Characteristics examined	Supplier's observations	Auditor findings
Anvil flatness	The micrometer anvil was checked for flatness at four quadrants with a 0.12500-inch precision ball and was found to be acceptable.	Auditor concurs with conclusions made by the supplier's calibration technician.
0.1000 inch	0.0999 inch*	0.1000 inch
0.2000 inch	0.1999 inch*	0.2000 inch
0.4500 inch	0.4499 inch*	0.4500 inch
0.7500 inch	0.7499 inch*	0.7500 inch
0.9500 inch	0.9499 inch*	0.9500 inch

----

*Records indicate that the variations from the instruments' nominal size as shown in column two were rectified by proper adjustments to the instruments. Since the tightest product tolerance associated with products produced is less than 0.001 inch, these variations do not have a negative impact on the acceptance or rejection of related product characteristics. The supplier did indicate, however, that this condition was directed to the attention of its material review board for review, concurrence, and to determine its impact on the adequacy of established calibration internals.

Vernier Caliper

Supporting Information

- Identification number: MI-301
- Discrimination: 0.001 inch
- Instrument accuracy: +/− 0.001 inch
- Instrument range: 0–12.000 inch
- Company standards consist of (a) precision gage blocks and (b) precision measuring rods.

Assessment

Assessments were made on calibration characteristics that were previously checked by the company's metrology specialist with measuring standards of known accuracy. The instruments were calibrated within an established calibration interval with standards traceable to NIST. The vernier caliper blade (measuring surface for external measurements) was examined for wear with a precision roll and found to be acceptable prior to making the following observations:

Characteristics examined	Standard used	Supplier's observations	Auditor findings
2.500 inch	Gage block	2.500 inch	2.500 inch
4.000 inch	Gage block	4.000 inch	4.000 inch
6.500 inch	Precision rod	6.500 inch	6.500 inch
8.000 inch	Precision rod	8.000 inch	8.000 inch
10.500 inch	Precision rod	10.500 inch	10.500 inch
12.00 inch	Precision rod	12.000 inch	12.500 inch

The audit report was submitted to the buying activity and a recommendation for a contract award regarding calibration capabilities was accepted.

Conclusion

Today more and more suppliers recognize that the establishment and maintenance of a calibration system is an imperative for verifying that products are produced right the first time. Many suppliers, however, fall short of documenting a satisfactory calibration system. This can be attributed to several causes. For example:

1. Some suppliers are simply not familiar with or are not aware of the calibration system standards and associated handbooks that are available to them from the American National Standards Institute, the American Society for Quality Control, and the International Organization for standardization.

2. Other suppliers are aware of these standards but elect to adopt only a portion or none of the applicable elements of an appropriate calibration system. In addition, improvements of deficiencies in the calibration system are normally made only after the receipt of deficiencies in the system that are detected and reported by internal and/or external customers.

3. There are also those offerers of products and services that have been in business for an extended period of time and are financially stable and are not motivated by any of its internal or external customers to establish and maintain an appropriate calibration system.

The American Society for Quality Control, the American National Standards Institute, and the International Organization for Standardization and their membership have made large contributions towards improving quality systems management nationally and internationally. For example, over the past two decades these organizations, with dedicated support from their membership, have published quality-related textbooks, standards, and technical papers. Their members regularly conduct seminars, conferences, and training programs for members as well as for the public in general. Lastly their ANSI/ISO/ASQC Q9000 certification program has brought and is continually bringing new offerers of products and services under their umbrella of registered and certified suppliers.

Notes

1. U.S. Department of Defense, General Services Administration, and National Aeronautics and Space Administration, *Government Federal Acquisition Regulation*, 1995, Part 9, clause 9.101.

Chapter 5

Communicating Calibration Capabilities: Using Effective Documentation

This chapter provides examples of quality-assurance data that are crucial in verifying the adequacy of an acceptable calibration system as well as for providing an indication of a supplier's calibration capabilities. The chapter includes sample documents in a case study format that demonstrate the use of documentation to monitor compliance with a calibration system requirement.

Abstract of Contract Quality Requirement

One of the most critical elements of a metrology system is the timely receipt of an all-inclusive abstract of contract quality requirements that clearly describe the statement of work and the assurance that applicable drawings, specifications, and standards are

From: Contract administrator

To: Quality-control manager

Subject: Contract quality requirements

1. Technical data
    a. Part name: shaft
    b. Quantity: 500 each
    c. Drawing (part number): ABC-123
    d. Inspection system requirements: ANSI/ISO/ASQC-Q9002
    e. Calibration system requirements: ISO-10012-1
    f. Product inspection site: place of production
    g. Product acceptance site: place of production
    h. Delivery schedule: 180 days (by 7/3/9X)
    i. F.O.B. point: Destination

2. Attachments
    a. Drawing number: ABC-123

3. Customer
    a. U.S. Government
       Naval Supply Center
       Norfolk, VA 23515

4. Comments: Specifications ANSI/ISO/ASQC-Q9002 referenced in the Abstract was furnished to the quality-control department under a previous abstract of contract quality requirements.

Figure 5.1   Abstract of contract quality requirement.

on hand or readily available when needed (see Figure 5.1). Each abstract or equivalent method of summarizing contract quality requirements, particularly for new and different product designs, should be reviewed in depth to assure that technical requirements are understood by the metrology manager and his/her staff of specialists. In addition, new product-designed requirements should be compared with previously prepared quality plans. Where a new product design has a direct impact on the metrology portion of a quality plan, these new requirements must be compared with previously prepared procedures and processes and tailored accordingly so as to meet new requirements.

Communication of contract quality requirements between the supplier's designated contract administrator and the manager of the metrology department (via the director of quality assurance) must be accomplished as early as possible so that

1. Where differences of opinions, ambiguity, or omissions prevail, they can be rectified without jeopardizing an established delivery schedule.
2. The metrology department will have sufficient lead time to review the complete technical package so that satisfactory planning can be accomplished right the first time.
3. The need for additional personnel, plant facilities, and inspection, testing, and measuring equipment can be determined.
4. The adequacy of existing policy, procedures, and processes can be identified.
5. Where appropriate, the capabilities of potential independent calibration laboratories and/or subcontractors can be identified.

Calibration records are essential for providing internal and external customers with an indication of a metrology department's ability to meet new calibration system requirements. They document the ability to maintain established policy procedures and processes. In addition, records provide an indication of instrument stability and reliability. A history of objective quality data forms the basis for the establishment or adjustment of calibration intervals. Records must be held in a manner that is readily available for use by management and operations personnel.

MASTER REQUIREMENTS LIST

From the abstract, the metrology manager or a designated representative will prepare a master requirements list (see Figure 5.2). The master requirements list is an important component of a supplier's overall quality plan, which is provided to the metrology

Product characteristic code number	Characteristic identification	Measuring device (MD)	MD identification number	MD code number
101	1.500″ + 0.000″ − 0.001″	1″–2″ Micrometer, outside	C10001	MD1
102	1.000″ + 0.000″ − 0.001″	1″ Micrometer, outside*	C10002	MD2
103	True position	Dial indicator	C10003	MD3
104	0.375 + 0.001″ − 0.000″	"Go/Not Go" plug gage	C10004	MD4
201	2.000″ +/− 0.005″	0″–6″ Vernier caliper	C10005	MD5
202	0.750″ +/− 0.005″	0″–6″ Vernier caliper	C10006	MD6
203	2.750 +/− 0.005″	0″–6″ Vernier caliper	C10007	MD7

Prepared by _____ Date _____

*For this characteristic, when the inspection process indicates that the manufactured product is larger than one inch, use a 1″–2″ micrometer to obtain the indicated measurement.

Figure 5.2   Master requirements list, number one, drawing ABC-123.

department for their planning and implementation. The list identifies product characteristics associated with a particular product design as well as the measuring instruments that are used to inspect the respective product characteristic. This list provides support to the quality data that is entered in the appropriate calibration and product observation records. The master requirements list in conjunction with an applicable product observation record (which also addresses an applicable purchase order or contract number) and a calibration record

Name of instrument	Nominal size	Accuracy value	Quantity	Application
Precision gage block set	*	*	1 set	**
Micrometer, outside	0"–1"	+/–0.0001"	1 each	***
Micrometer, outside	0"–2"	+/–0.0001"	1 each	***
Dial indicator	0"–0.005"	+/–0.0001"	1 each	***
"Go/Not Go" plug gage	0.375"	+/–0.0001"	1 each	***
Vernier caliper	0"–6"	+/–0.001"	1 each	***

*Refer to certificate of calibration located in the respective gage block set container
**Measurement standard
***Product inspection

Figure 5.3   Calibration equipment list.

completes the traceability loop. It simplifies the investigation of customer complaints and becomes the initial focus for the investigation of justified customer complaints.

CALIBRATION EQUIPMENT LIST

Following the review of technical documents associated with a specific contract, the metrology manager, in concert with the quality-control manager, prepares a listing of measurement standards and working instruments that are required for all metrology operations. This list includes all instruments used to make required measurements or used to calibrate regardless of ownership (see Figure 5.3). By establishing and maintaining inventory lists of both active as well as inactive inspection, measuring, and test equipment, quality-assurance personnel are able to prepare a master quality plan for each new product design. The lists also support the individual planning and application of individual calibration technicians. These lists provide management and operations personnel with ready access to information that is critical to the

1. Availability of inspection, measuring, and test equipment that may or may not be required by a new product design
2. Need for inactive instruments to be calibrated and transferred to the active list of calibrated M&TE
3. Assessment of whether instruments in current inventory have the required accuracies required by the new product design
4. Assessment of the need to upgrade existing calibration procedures
5. Assessment of the need to establish new calibration procedures

The following factors should be addressed when preparing an instrument inventory list:

1. Instrument nomenclature
2. Number of identical instruments
3. Product manufacturer's instrument identification number
4. Instrument manufacturer's instrument identification number
5. Instrument discrimination
6. Instrument accuracy
7. Description of use

CALIBRATION PROCEDURES
FOR MEASURING AND TEST EQUIPMENT

The primary purpose of preparing calibration procedures is to provide metrology personnel with a detailed description of how to perform calibrations of each inspection, measuring, and testing device that is used within the system. The procedures identify the standards that will be used to verify the accuracy of the calibrated working instruments. In addition to a step-by-step calibration procedure, calibration instructions should address

Instrument nomenclature: micrometer, outside, 1"–2"
Identification number: C10001
Calibration procedure number: CP-1
Instrument accuracy: +/– 0.0001"
Discrimination: 0.0001"
Range of instrument: 1"–2"
Measurement standard required: precision gage block set
Accuracy of measurement standard: refer to certified calibration record for accuracy values

Calibration process:

- The instrument shall be calibrated in a room having a temperature between 65° F and 75° F, +/– 5° F. The temperature shall be stabilized and shall remain constant during the calibration process. The room must be dust- and particle-free during the calibration process.

- Visually examine the instrument for damage prior to calibration.

- Clean the instrument's measuring surfaces with a lint-free cloth prior to the start of calibration.

- Check the micrometer over gage blocks 1.000", 1.250", 1.750", and 2.000".

- When measured readings exceed the accuracy tolerance of the micrometer measurement, remove the instrument from service for adjustment and recalibration.

- Document calibration results on the calibration form.

- Out-of-tolerance conditions should be documented on the metrology deficiency report form and brought to the attention of the quality-control manager for necessary action.

- Attach a calibration status label to the instrument and its container.

Prepared by _____ Date _____

Approved by _____ Date _____

Figure 5.4   Calibration procedure for micrometer , 1–2 inches.

1. The accuracy tolerance of calibrated instruments
2. The area of uncertainty of measurement standards as well as the area of uncertainty of the characteristic being calibrated
3. The accuracy ratio between the measurement standard and the characteristic being calibrated

Calibration procedures are required for the measuring devices referenced on the master requirements list (see Figures 5.4, 5.5, 5.6, 5.7, and 5.8).

Instrument nomenclature: micrometer, outside, 0"–1"
Identification number: C10002
Calibration procedure number: CP-2
Instrument accuracy: +/– 0.0001"
Discrimination: 0.0001"
Range: 0"–1"
Measurement standard required:

    a. Precision gage block set
        Accuracy of measurement standard: refer to certified calibration
        record for accuracy values
    b. Precision measuring ball: 12500"
        Accuracy: 0.0002"

Calibration process:

- The instrument must be calibrated in a room having a temperature between 65° F and 75° F that should remain constant during the calibration process.

- The calibration area must be dust- and particle-free during the calibration process.

- Visually examine the instrument for damage before calibration.

- Clean the instrument's measuring surface with a lint-free cloth prior to the start of calibration.

- Check the micrometer anvil (measuring surface) with a 0.125" precision measuring ball for flatness at four quadrants. Remove the micrometer from service for repair, recalibration, or replacement when the flatness exceeds 0.0002".

- Take measurements on the instrument at five places over precision gage blocks 0.100", 0.375", 0.500", 0.750", and 1.000". When measured readings exceed the accuracy tolerance of the micrometer measurements, remove the instrument from service for adjustment and/or repair.

- Document calibration results on the calibration form.

- Document out-of-tolerance conditions on the metrology deficiency report form and bring to the attention of the quality-control manager.

- Attach a calibration status label to the instrument and its container.

Prepared by _____ Date _____

Approved by _____ Date _____

Figure 5.5   Calibration procedure for micrometer , 0–1 inch.

Instrument nomenclature: dial indicator
Identification number: C10003
Calibration procedure number: CP-3
Instrument accuracy: +/– 0.0001″
Discrimination: 0.0001″
Range of instrument: 0″–0.005″
Measurement standard required: precision gage block set
Accuracy of measurement standard: refer to certified calibration record for accuracy values

Calibration process:

- The instrument should be calibrated in a room having a temperature between 65° F and 75° F that must remain constant during the calibration process.

- The calibration area must be dust- and particle-free during the calibration process.

- Visually examine the instrument for damage before calibrating the instrument and verify that the shaft that initiates the dial movement moves freely. If the shaft does not move freely, remove the dial indicator from service for repair and/or replacement.

- Clean all measuring surfaces with a lint-free cloth before the start of calibration.

- Required equipment:
  a. Surface plate
  b. Parallel bar
  c. Precision gage block set
  d. Height gage mounting fixture

- Proceed as follows:
  a. Zero the dial indicator over a 0.100″ gage block.
  b. Take measurements over gage blocks 0.101″, 0.102″, 0.103″, 0.104″, and 0.105″.

- When measured value exceeds the specified accuracy of the dial indicator, remove the instrument from service for repair, recalibration, or replacement.

- Document calibration results on the calibration form.

- Out-of-tolerance conditions should be documented on the metrology deficiency report form and brought to the attention of the quality-control manager for necessary action.

- Attach a calibration status label to the instrument and its container.

Prepared by _____ Date _____

Approved by _____ Date _____

Figure 5.6   Calibration procedure for dial indicator.

Instrument nomenclature: "Go/Not Go" plug gage
Identification number: C10004
Calibration procedure number: CP-4
Accuracy of plug gage: 0.0002"
Measurement standards required:
   a. Precision gage block set
   b. Bench micrometer with 0.000050" discrimination

Calibration process:

■ The gage shall be calibrated in a room having a temperature between 65° F and 75° F, +/– 5° F. The temperature must be stabilized and remain constant during the calibration process.

■ The room must be dust- and particle-free during the calibration process.

■ Visually examine the instrument for damage prior to calibration.

■ Clean the instrument's measuring surfaces with a lint-free cloth prior to the start of calibration.

■ Place the bench micrometer on a surface plate and set it up with a gage block that represents the size of the plug that is being calibrated.

■ Measure the "Go" member of the gage as well as the "Not Go" member at six locations, front, middle, and back, taking three readings at 0° and three readings at 90°.

■ When the measured value exceeds the specified accuracy requirements, the plug will be removed from service and either returned to the instrument manufacturer for rework to specified accuracy requirements or scrapped.

■ Document calibration results on the calibration form.

■ Out-of-tolerance conditions should be documented on the metrology deficiency report form and brought to the attention of the quality-control manager for necessary action.

■ Attach a calibration status label to the instrument as well as to the instrument's container.

Prepared by _____ Date _____

Approved by _____ Date _____

Figure 5.7   Calibration procedure for "Go/Not Go" plug gage.

PRODUCT OBSERVATION RECORDS FOR M&TE

The observation record of product inspection (see Figure 5.9) contains the following additional factors that pertain to the product and instrument traceability loop:

Instrument nomenclature: vernier caliper
Identification number: C10005
Calibration procedure number: CP-5
Instrument accuracy: +/– 0.0001"
Discrimination: 0.0001"
Range: 0"–6"
Measurement standard required: precision gage block set

Calibration process:

- The instrument shall be calibrated in a room having a temperature between 65° F and 75° F, +/– 5° F. The temperature shall be stabilized and shall remain constant during the calibration process.

- The room must be dust-free during the calibration process.

- Visually examine the instrument for damage prior to calibration.

- Clean the instrument's measuring surface with a lint-free cloth prior to the start of calibration.

- Check the vernier's wear jaw by visual means and by taking measurements over a gage pin or ring gage at the front, middle, and back side of the wear jaw.

- Check measurements on the vernier caliper over gage block sizes 0.500", 0.750", 2.000", 4.000", and 6.000".

- Document calibration results on the calibration form provided for this purpose.

- Out-of-tolerance conditions shall be documented on the metrology deficiency report form and brought to the attention of the quality-control manager for necessary action.

- Attach a calibration status label to the instrument as well as to its container.

Prepared by _____ Date _____

Approved by _____ Date _____

Figure 5.8   Calibration procedure for vernier caliper.

1. Master requirements list code number   This number identifies the appropriate number that can be traceable to a specific master requirements list assigned to a specific product.

2. Product characteristic code number   This number identifies the product characteristic in question, which is listed on the master requirements list

3. Measurement device code number   This number identifies the specific measuring device that was used to check the particular product characteristic in question.

Observation Record

Item description ___Shaft___ Dwg. no. ___ABC-123___

Spec. no. ___N/A___ Other ___

Insp. station	Purchase order or contract number	Sampling plan: ANSI/ASQ Z1.4 N-II-S	Julian date	Revision no.	Lot size	Sample size	Accept no.	Reject no.	M/req. list no.	101 (MD1)	102 (MD2)	103 (MD3)	104 (MD4)	201 (MD5)	202 (MD5)	203 (MD5)	No. obs.	No. def. obs.	% Defective	Disposition	Inspector
5	123xxxxxx	Major 1.5	66	—	500	50	2	3	1	0	50/4	50/0	50/0				200	4	2	R	SI
5	123xxxxxx	Minor 4.0	66	—	—	50	7	8	1	—	—	—	—				150	0	0	A	SI
11	123xxxxxx	Resubmitted								50/0	50/0	50/0	50/0				200	0	0	A	SI
11	123xxxxxx	Lot —												50/0	50/0	50/0	150	0	0	A	SI

Character and Measuring Device Code Number

1: SPC program   2: Receiving inspection   3: First article inspection   4: In-process inspection   5: Final inspection   6: Shipping inspection

Figure 5.9   Sample observation record of product inspection.

Other pertinent information listed in the observation record of product inspection that must be considered when accessing traceability information referenced therein includes the actual measurement(s) listed in the observation record that should be compared with the values referenced in a customer complaint and the purchase order or contract, as appropriate.

METROLOGY DEFICIENCY REPORT

Significant out-of-tolerance conditions are reported to the metrology manager by the calibration technicians and, where appropriate, to other department managers that depend on the use of M&TE of known accuracy. This report alerts the metrology manager to take immediate corrective action to preclude any further acceptance of products using inspection, measuring, and test equipment with questionable accuracy.

NONCONFORMING PRODUCT REPORT

This report is issued to preclude the repetitive acceptance of nonconforming products and services, to take satisfactory corrective action, to identify the assignable cause, and to determine if the complaint is related to instruments with questionable accuracy.

EVIDENCE OF CAPABILITY

The process of establishing objective quality evidence regarding calibration capability that will meet the interests of a product manufacturer and/or an independent calibration laboratory as well as the expectation of customers starts with contract quality requirements that are clearly communicated from the purchaser to the supplier of a product or service and from the supplier to the metrology department. Clearly communicated contract quality requirements beget a robust quality plan. It is from the quality plan or, where appropriate, from an abstract of contract quality or a combination of both where required measuring instruments are identified (see Figures 5.1 and 5.10).

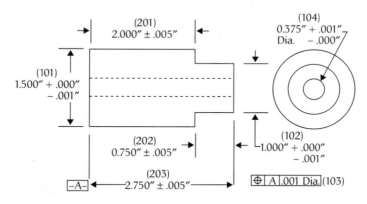

Part name: shaft
Part number: ABC-123
Characteristic codes:
                    Major: 101–104
                    Minor: 201–203

Figure 5.10   Abstract of solicitation requirements.

USING THE SAMPLE DOCUMENTS

An observation (product) record is included in this chapter for the purpose of establishing a process for tracing a defective product characteristic to the specific measuring device that was used to check a defective product characteristic (see Figure 5.9). This operation is one of the important steps that are required in the corrective action process.

The first step in the traceability process is to identify the master requirements list (see Figure 5.2) that pertains to the product characteristic in question. This number may be found in the tenth block from the left on the observation record. The master requirements list will provide the necessary information to satisfactorily investigate the cause, which is crucial to preclude the recurrence of the reported deficiency.

If the deficiency is found to be related to the measuring device, then focus will be centered on correcting the out-of-tolerance condition of the respective measuring device. If the pertinent

To: Metrology manager

From: Calibration technician

Report number: 1

Date: 2/11/9X

Measuring device: micrometer, outside, one inch

Instrument identification number: C100002

Calibration procedure number: CP-2

Reply due date: 2/18/9X

Signature of requestor: S/J. McTechnician

Out-of-tolerance condition: Measured values for characteristic 0.001"–1.000" have drifted from their nominal size by 0.00005." While this is still an in-tolerance condition, it indicates a trend toward an out-of-tolerance condition.

Corrective action reply as to cause: Normal wear trend

Recommended action: Continue to calibrate weekly and do not proceed to a revised calibration frequency until the conditions of the calibration system manual are met.

Investigator's signature: S/J. McMetrology

Title: Metrology manager

Date: 2/15/9X

Figure 5.11   Metrology deficiency report.

measuring instrument is found to be in tolerance, then the investigation will be directed to the processes that were used to produce the product.

The metrology deficiency report (see Figure 5.11) is used for reporting out-of-tolerance conditions. The information contained in this example is associated with the 2/11/9X entry shown under "Work Performance," on the calibration record (see Figure 5.12).

Investigation results regarding the inadequacy of the processes that were used to manufacture the product are documented on the nonconforming material report (see Figure 5.13).

─── **Calibration Record** ───

Instrument Micrometer, outside, one inch

Model N/A   Location Final inspection

I.d. no. C10002   Accuracy +/− 0.0001 "

Procedure no. CP-2   Discrimination 0.0001 "

Calibration freq. P*   Tamper-proof ☐ Yes   ☒ No

Other *Prior to use

Date calibrated	Due date	Calibration technician	.001 "	.375 "	.500 "	.750 "	1.000 "	Anvil	Vis.			
			Work performance — Characteristic identification → Measured value									
1/10/9x	P	JM	.001	.375	.500	.750	1.000	ok	ok			
1/11/9x	P	JM	.001	.375	.500	.750	1.000	ok	ok			
1/12/9x	P	JM	.001	.375	.500	.750	1.000	ok	ok			
1/13/9x	P	JM	.001	.375	.500	.750	1.000	ok	ok			
1/14/9x	Change freq. to weekly		−	−	−	−	−	−	−			
1/21/9x	1/28/9x	JM	.001	.375	.500	.750	1.000	ok	ok			
1/28/9x	2/4/9x	JM	.001	.375	.500	.750	1.000	ok	ok			
2/4/9x	2/11/9x	JM	.001	.375	.500	.750	1.000	ok	ok			
2/11/9x	2/18/9x	JM	.09995	.37495	.49995	.74995	.99995	ok	ok			

Figure 5.12   Sample calibration record of M&TE.

Distribution: _____ Report number _____

Quality control manager _____ Engineering _____ Plant manager _____

With production lot _____ Other _____

Part name: shaft   Part number: ABC–123   Job number: JN-100

Sampling plan:
ANSI/ASQC Z1.4, normal inspection, Level II, single sampling acceptable quality level-1.0 major characteristics and 4.0 for minor characteristics

Quantity accepted: none   Quantity rejected: 500 each

Contract number: N68335-XX-X-XXXX

Description of defect:
Characteristic 1.000" + 0.0000" and –0.001 code number 102 measures 1.001" which is oversize by 0.001".

Cause of the defect:
Examination of the machine that produced the part indicates that the cutting tool is worn. The production lot returned to the manufacturing department for screening and rework.

Corrective action taken:
a. Worn cutting tool replaced with a new one.
b. Defective parts reworked to drawing requirement.
c. Production lot resubmitted to the inspection department and all drawing characteristics reinspected and were found to be in compliance with drawing requirements.
d. A recheck of the micrometer that was used to check the part indicates that it was within the instrument's accuracy requirements.

Signature _____ Title _____ Date _____

Figure 5.13   Nonconforming material report.

Metrology managers who establish a uniform policy, assign responsibilities, and provide their team of calibration technicians with robust procedures and processes will experience little or no difficulty in convincing second- or third-party quality assessors that they have administrative and technical capabilities. When providers of products and services demonstrate that they have both administrative and technical capabilities they provide to internal and external managers assurance that the probability of product rejections, production delays, late deliveries of products and services, customer complaints, and losses will be minimized.

CHAPTER 6

Case Study 2—Supplier's Calibration System: An Integral Part of an ANSI/ISO/ASQC Q9000 Quality System Manual

The selection and application of an appropriate calibration system standard is based on a supplier's own initiative in anticipation of contracts that specify a requirement for the establishment and maintenance of an acceptable calibration system. A system is selected to meet the needs, interests, and expectations of internal and external customers. For this case study the focus is centered on ISO 10012-1, 1992, Quality Assurance Requirements for Measuring Equipment—Part 1: Metrological Confirmation System for Measuring Equipment.

During the past two decades several new calibration system standards were introduced to the public by the United States and the world community. All of these standards, including U.S. Department of Defense Mil-Std 45662A Calibration System Standard, which is now being overshadowed by the new standards published by the American National Institute (ANSI),

XXX Company, Inc.
Anytown, USA
Calibration System Procedure

Prepared by* _____ Title _____ Date _____
(Signature)

Reviewed by** _____ Title _____ Date _____

Approved by: *** _____ Title _____ Date _____

Distribution:

Copy No.	Recipient
1	Master file
2	Director of quality assurance
3	Metrology manager
4	Customer

  * Metrology manager
 ** Director of quality assurance
*** Plant manager

Figure 6.1   Signatures of key quality management personnel.

the International Organization for Standardization (ISO), and the American Society for Quality Control (ASQC) provide the supplier with guidance regarding the establishment and maintenance of associated policies and procedures.

Standards include ISO 10012-1, 1992, ANSI/ASQC M1— American National Standard for Calibration Systems 1987; American National Standards for Calibration, Calibration Laboratories and Measuring and Test Equipment—General Requirements, ANSI/NCSL-Z540-1, 1994; ISO/IEC Guide 25, General Requirements for the Competence of Calibration and Testing Laboratories, 1990; or Mil Std 45662A Calibration System Requirements. It is important to note with all standards that since the information contained in these standards essentially provides the same message, suppliers of metrology services may tailor an existing calibration policy to meet any of these calibration system standards or to address supplementary specification requirements. Examples of such supplementary requirements might include concurrent calibration of measuring instruments between customer and supplier quality-assurance representatives or identifying the responsibility and processes for the recalibration of customer-supplied M&TE.

MANAGEMENT'S COMMITMENT TO QUALITY EXCELLENCE

To meet the needs, interests, and expectations of both internal and external customers starting with the implementation, maintenance, and continuous improvement of the policies and procedures referenced herein.

John Q. Quality, CEO
XXX Company, Inc.

Table of Contents

Topic	Section

RECORD OF CHANGES

Date	Revisions, additions, and deletions
5/7/9X	1. Deleted all references to Mil Std 45662A
	2. Added in its place ISO standard 10012-1, Quality Assurance Requirements of Measuring Equipment—Part 1: Metrological Confirmation for Measuring Equipment

OVERVIEW OF THE CONFIRMATION SYSTEM[1]

The XXX Company is a medium-size company staffed with approximately 200 employees that produce mechanical and electromechanical equipment. The company's calibration laboratory, which is the primary source for the calibration of M&TE and secondary standards, is headed by a metrology manager, who reports directly to the director of quality assurance, and a staff of calibration technicians.

Independent calibration laboratories are solicited to calibrate our MS and to repair and recalibrate some M&TE. The policies and procedures described herein are issued to control the accuracy of M&TE in accordance with the intent of the International Organization for Standardization (ISO) 10012-1, Quality Assurance Requirements for Measuring Equipment—Part 1: Metrological Configuration System for Measuring Equipment.

The accuracy of all inspection, measuring, and test equipment used to inspect and test products and services and to assess process improvement techniques is calibrated with higher-level standards of known accuracy. New M&TE is calibrated when the instrument is introduced into the calibration system. These instruments are continually calibrated prior to use until sufficient data is generated to justify an established frequency of recalibration giving due consideration to the instruments' stability, purpose, discrimination, and degree of usage. The results of each calibration will be entered into our computer system for subsequent statistical analysis, detection of accuracy trends, and the adjustment of calibration intervals where appropriate.

Inventory Record of M&TE and MS

An inventory record of all active and inactive measuring instruments, consisting of the following information, is located in a separate calibration procedures manual:

- Instrument nomenclature
- Instrument identification number
- Instrument description and use
- Nominal value

- Accuracy of certified value
- Source of calibration
- Standard procedures
- Instrument manufacturer's written instructions
- Company prepared instructions
- Calibration procedure number

Inactive or uncalibrated instruments are identified as such and they are stored in an area separate and apart from active gages.

The director of quality assurance with support from auditors periodically reviews established procedures and processes to verify that they contain complete details for meeting current and future specified requirements of the ISO 100012-1 standard. New customer requirements and recommendations that will improve process management which exceed the procedures covered herein, along with recommendations from our internal customers, will be established and implemented as an interim change. Interim changes and other improvements will be included in the basic quality manual during the annual revision of the complete manual. No changes are valid until they are reviewed by the director of quality assurance and approved by the plant manager. Where there is a need for new and unfamiliar inspection and test equipment, particularly during product design development, personnel will be provided with necessary training to use the new measuring equipment prior to production of products and services offered to the customer. Only those gages that are properly calibrated shall be made available for use at the respective verification station. Objective quality evidence regarding the accuracy of M&TE and primary and secondary standards shall be made available for review and assessment by the purchaser when so requested.

PLANNING[2]

Calibration systems planning is accomplished by the director of quality assurance, the metrology manager, and their staff technicians.

Current Contracts

For add-on contracts associated with products currently produced by our company, focus shall be centered on whether established policy and processes are up-to-date and readily available when needed.

New Contracts for New Product Designs

For product designs that are new to our company, the metrology manager will be furnished with a list of all drawings, specifications, standards, an abstract of contract quality requirements, and a copy of an established quality plan. The metrology manager shall then determine via the review of these documents specified product tolerances, M&TE accuracy requirements, and the availability of associate M&TE and MS from company inventory.

Where additional instruments are to be purchased from an outside source, the metrology manager shall include the pertinent calibration system standard requirements and a certified statement regarding the traceability of the supplier's measurement standards to the National Institute of Standards and Technology (NIST) in his/her requisition to the purchasing manager. The certification shall also be supported with objective quality evidence.

Delivery of calibrated instruments, that is in consonance with our company's established milestone schedules shall be included in the purchase order.

Periodic Audit and Review of the Confirmation System[3]

Audits of company procedures, processes, and personnel who implement the calibration system are carried out by a person or a team of calibration specialists familiar with our established policies and procedures. Such a person, or persons, may be an employee or an accredited third party *not* having specific responsibilities in the department audited.

Frequency of Audits

Scheduled audits for all departments that support calibration systems management are conducted at least once a year. Unscheduled audits that are performed more frequently than once a year are motivated by contract change notices, continuous process improvement recommendations, and customer complaints.

Reports

Reports regarding audit observations are documented and reported to the director of quality assurance with appropriate recommendations for process improvements. The director of quality assurance will assure that audit recommendations for improvements are implemented and properly maintained.

Measuring Equipment[4]
Measurement Standards

Standards used by an independent calibration laboratory to calibrate our company's standards shall have the accuracy, stability, range, and resolution to assure that required measurement areas of acceptance are maintained.

Traceability

Independent laboratory standards that are used to calibrate our measuring equipment shall have a higher-level of accuracy of at least 10 times greater than our working standards. Primary and secondary standards are traceable by an unbroken chain of calibration events to the National Institute of Standards and Technology (NIST) or an international standard.

The accuracy of the company's standards are 10 times greater than the accuracy of our M&TE and are traceable to NIST. Accuracy ratios between the M&TE that is used to inspect and test product are 4:1 or greater than the products' tightest tolerance. (Note: Specific accuracy ratios are contained in the instrument's calibration procedure.)

Uncertainty of Measurements[5]

(Accuracy ratios of area of acceptance and area of uncertainty)

Laboratory Standards

All of the company's standards are calibrated by an independent calibration laboratory with known capabilities. The metrology manager will assure that our purchase orders will include, in the statement of work, that company standards will be calibrated with higher-level standards with an accuracy ratio of at least 10 times better than the instrument being calibrated with an area of uncertainty no greater than 10 percent. The statement of work also includes requirements for the independent calibration laboratory to furnish a certified calibration report showing a list of actual measurements and the actual area (value) of uncertainty.

The metrology manager or his/her designated representative reviews the laboratory's certificate and documents evidence of acceptance (or nonacceptance) by applying his/her signature or inspection stamp to the certificate.

Company Standards

The accuracy ratio between our measurement standards and our M&TE shall be 10:1. Company standards that are found to have an area of uncertainty greater than 10 percent are replaced with a standard that is in compliance with the pertinent calibration procedure. The replaced standard will be repaired, where appropriate, and recalibrated or downgraded.

M&TE and Product Tolerance

The area of uncertainty of working M&TE in relation to an associated product characteristic tolerance is in accordance with the appropriate quality plan. The area of uncertainty shall be between 10 and 25 percent. Technicians and inspectors refer to the applicable product and calibration procedure when determining the appropriate accuracy ratio between instrument accuracy and the product tolerance. When calibration data show a negative trend in

an area of uncertainty, the metrology manager or his/her designated representative shall investigate the cause of this trend and
take appropriate action.

CUMULATIVE EFFECT OF UNCERTAINTIES[6]

All calibration procedures shall address the cumulative effect that
the instrument's area of uncertainty has on products and services
produced for our customers. The cumulative effect of the uncer-
tainties regarding each stage of the chain of calibrations from primary through secondary standards to working M&TE to the
product tolerance shall be maintained as follows:

• The accuracy ratio between laboratory standards and our
  company standards secondary shall be 10:1 or greater.
• The accuracy ratio between company standards and working
  M&TE shall be 10:1 or greater.

The accuracy ratio between the company's inspection, measuring, and test equipment and the product tolerance shall be
from 4:1 to 10:1. (Selected accuracy ratios or modifications
thereto are contained in the respective quality plan.) When an
area of uncertainty is found to be greater than the value specified
in the respective calibration procedure (or one that is found to
have an area of acceptance less than the value specified in the calibration procedure), the instrument shall be removed from the
calibration area and recalibrated followed by an investigation as
to its impact on the products and services that were previously re-
leased to the next operation, to storage, to the shipping department, or to the customer/user. For example:

1. A working instrument with an accuracy ratio of 4:1 and an area
   of uncertainty found to be greater than 25 percent will require
   an investigation to determine the adequacy of established
   calibration procedures as well as the quality status of products
   and services previously accepted.

2. A standard instrument with an accuracy ratio of 10:1 and an
    area of uncertainty is found to be greater than 10 percent will
    require an investigation to determine the adequacy of
    established calibration procedures as well as to verify the
    accuracy of M&TE previously calibrated.

DOCUMENTED CONFIRMATION PROCEDURES[7]

There are three sources of calibration procedures that are used by
our company.

1. Standard calibration procedures that are available from the
    Government Industry Data Exchange Program (GIDEP)
2. Instrument manufacturer's recommended calibration
    procedures
3. Company-prepared procedures

Calibration procedures prepared by our company shall include
the following:

- Original/revision date
- Instrument nomenclature
- Calibration procedure number
- Accuracy of instrument to be calibrated
- Instrument range
- Instrument discrimination
- Measurement standard(s)
- Step-by-step procedure
- Name of originator/title/date

RECORDS[8]

Records are contained on the following documents:

1. An abstract of contract quality requirements, which includes:
    - Contract or purchase order number
    - Contract or purchase order change notices

- Description of supplies and services solicited/offered
- First article where appropriate, and delivery date
- Concurrent inspection and acceptance with the customer's quality-assurance representative, where appropriate
- Item number
- Quantity
- Delivery date(s)
- Copy of, or source of, drawings, specifications, standards, and other contract quality requirements such as tailoring and supplementary requirements
- Name of the originator of the abstract, title, and date

2. Calibration equipment list, which includes:
   - Name of the instrument
   - Nominal size
   - Accuracy value
   - Quantity
   - Application (primary or secondary standard or working M&TE)

3. Master requirements list, which includes:
   - Product nomenclature and part number
   - Product characteristic code number
   - Measuring device used to inspect/test the product
   - Measuring device identification number
   - Measuring device code number

4. Instrument calibration record, which includes:
   - Instrument nomenclature
   - Model number
   - Identification number
   - Accuracy of the instrument
   - Procedure number
   - Resolution value
   - Calibration frequency
   - Characteristic identification

- Work performance
- Characteristic identification
- Measured value

5. Observation record, which includes but is not limited to:
   - Product characteristics and/or code number
   - Measuring device that was used to check the product characteristic
   - Measuring device code number

6. Recall/location record, which includes:
   - Instrument nomenclature
   - Identification number
   - Calibration frequency
   - Item location
   - Date recalled
   - Calibration date
   - Assigned to
   - Date in service
   - Assigned by
   - Remarks as appropriate

7. Calibration status labels, which include:
   - Last calibration date
   - Calibration due date
   - Calibrated by

8. Nonconforming M&TE tag, which identifies:
   - Date
   - Department
   - Instrument nomenclature
   - Instrument identification number
   - Quantity
   - Instruments that are out-of-tolerance
   - Brief description of out-of-tolerance condition
   - Associated contract or purchase order number
   - Signature and date of person who originated the complaint

9. Metrology deficiency report, which includes:
   - Instrument nomenclature
   - Originator of the report
   - Recipient of the report
   - Report number and date
   - Description of the measuring device
   - Calibration procedure number
   - Reply due date
   - Signature of the originator
   - Description of the out-of-tolerance condition
   - Reply as to cause
   - Recommended action
   - Investigator's signature/title/date
10. Material review board (MRB) report, which includes:
    - Instrument identification number
    - Product name and identification number
    - Specification number
    - Drawing number
    - Calibration procedure number
    - Number of instruments reported out-of-tolerance
    - Department and verification station
    - Vendor (where appropriate)
    - Description of complaint
    - Frequency of the complaint
    - Originator of the complaint
    - Date complaint submitted to MRB
    - Name and title of MRB members
    - Assignment of recommended corrective action
    - Action required
    - Follow up date
    - Signatures and title of MRB members

- Recipient of information copies of MRB findings to key management personnel

11. Corrective action record, which includes:
    - Originator of the request for corrective action
    - Recipient of the information
    - Instrument nomenclature and identification number
    - Number of instruments received
    - Number of defective instruments
    - Disposition

12. Vendor performance history, which includes:
    - ANSI/ISO/ASQC/Q9000 registered and certified
    - Distribution to personnel who have a need to know
    - Name and address of the vendor being tracked
    - Date capabilities originally verified
    - Record of past performance
    - Date
    - Contract or purchase order number
    - Instrument identification number
    - Quantity rejected
    - Comments (enter as appropriate)
    - Vendor is qualified
    - Corrective action required
    - Seek other sources

13. Employee training record (metrology)
    - Employee name, date, and address
    - Calibration capabilities
    - Calibration systems management capabilities
    - Required company training
    - List of skills and years of experience
    - Future training plans
    - Training monitor

Nonconforming Measuring Equipment[9]

A record of M&TE that is out-of-tolerance will be clearly identified on a nonconforming M&TE tag. The information contained on this tag shall include the date, quantity, department, instrument identification number, brief description of nonconformity, associated contract or purchase order number, and the signature and title of the person who reported the complaint.

Company M&TE

All nonconforming instruments will be placed in a designated holding area specifically selected for discrepant instruments. No one is authorized to remove nonconforming instruments from the holding area until satisfactory corrective action is taken by the metrology manager who is responsible for preliminary review (PR) actions, with assistance from other calibration technicians, when the out-of-tolerance condition is initially discovered and, where appropriate, prior to referral to the material review board for disposition. The material review board shall support the corrective action process and the disposition of nonconforming instruments where the complaint involves products and services previously accepted with instruments of questionable accuracy.

Significant out-of-tolerance conditions, which adversely affect product and service quality, shall be documented on a metrology deficiency report form (see Figure 5.11) and corrected within 10 working days. Follow-up action shall be taken by the metrology manager to verify satisfactory implementation of recommended corrective action. This action shall be taken within seven days after resolution of the deficiency.

Inspection and Test Equipment Furnished to Subcontractors

When complaints are received from subcontractors regarding the receipt of out-of-tolerance M&TE furnished by our company, an immediate investigation will be taken by our customer-complaint department representative to determine if the complaint is justified. Where a complaint is found to be justified the following actions shall be taken:

- Examine company calibration records for any indication of nonconformity and at the same time request that the instrument be returned to our company for our assessment and necessary action
- If this is not practical, arrangements shall be made for an investigation of the complaint by a representative of our metrology department at the subcontractor's facility where the instrument in question is located.
- Recalibrate the instrument to determine actual out-of-tolerance conditions
- Submit a report of findings to the director of quality assurance
- Recalibrate the instrument or replace it with one of known accuracy
- Determine the adequacy of established calibration procedures
- Determine if calibration intervals should be shortened
- Determine if the instrument should be calibrated prior to use

If the reported complaint was detected after product and service assessments, determine the impact that the out-of-tolerance condition has on products and services accepted with instruments in question. Follow-up action shall be taken by the quality assurance department on corrective action taken on internal and external complaints to verify that satisfactory corrective action was taken.

CONFIRMATION LABELING[10]

M&TE used to inspect/test products and services offered to our customers are identified as to their confirmation status. Where practical, the following information shall be referenced on each label or tags:

- Date of calibration
- Due date for next calibration

- Calibrated by
- Tags/labels associated with "limited use" instruments are identified with the action range calibrated
- Person responsible for confirmation
- Compensating correction factors, where appropriate

Where it is not practical to label an instrument, the confirmation status shall be identified on its container. Color coding is used instead of labels or tags when the small size or functional characteristics of the instrument precludes container marking, labels, or tags. Color coding provides only the year and month that the instrument is due for recalibration.

Confirmation Due Date Color Codes

Year	Color code (first dot)
19XX	Silver
19XX	Gold
19XX	White
20XX	Violet
20XX	Blue
20XX	Green
20XX	Gray
20XX	Orange
20XX	Yellow
20XX	Red
20XX	Brown
20XX	Black

Month	Color code (second dot)
January	Black
February	Brown
March	Red

April	Yellow
May	Orange
June	Gray
July	Green
August	Blue
September	Violet
October	White
November	Gold
December	Silver

Due date: Exact due date for calibration is contained in the respective calibration procedure.

Computer-generated data listing instrument nomenclature, identification numbers, and their calibration due dates are furnished to technicians on the first working day of the month for review and identification of exact calibration due dates. Obsolete and out-of service instruments will be placed in a locked storage cabinet and/or storage area and identified as such to assure that uncalibrated measuring equipment will not be used until properly calibrated. Personally owned M&TE, which include employee and independent consultant/laboratory instruments, will be used only when approved by the quality control manager.

When the use of personally owned equipment is authorized for acceptance purposes, the equipment will be labeled in accordance with established company policy and maintained in accordance with procedures referenced herein.

Externally calibrated M&TE will be identified in accordance with the statement of work provisions referenced in the contract/purchase order.

Sealing for Integrity[11]

Tamper-resistant seals shall be affixed to operator-accessible adjustments on M&TE and MS that, if moved, will affect the calibration. The director of quality assurance and, where appropriate, with support from the customer's quality assurance representative shall identify instruments that require seals based on their experience regarding how the instruments are used in support of contract quality requirements. The calibration technician/agency shall verify that instruments are removed from use if the seals are found to be broken.

INTERVALS OF CONFIRMATION[12]

Intervals of confirmation of M&TE and MS are assigned and maintained by the metrology manager and his/her staff of calibration technicians. The intervals are based on stability, purpose, and degree of usage. A listing of measurement standards and working instruments is located in the company's procedures manual. Instruments are always calibrated with higher-level standards of known accuracy and each unit of M&TE is calibrated prior to use when

1. First introduced to the calibration system
2. They are inactive over an extended period of time
3. There is evidence of damage or mishandling

The introduction of a calibration interval is predicated on objective quality evidence generated during previous calibrations. Intervals of confirmation shall be shortened only when the record reflects a favorable calibration history. A recall system is maintained by the metrology department to assure that active instruments will be calibrated prior to use or in accordance with an established calibration frequency. The recall record is maintained on the respective recall/location form (see Figure 2.4).

Regarding instruments that are on an established interval of confirmation, department supervisors will be notified of instruments that are overdue for recalibration via internal communication procedures (e-mail, memos, etc.). (Note: A temporary extension of calibration due dates may be authorized only when a favorable in-tolerance history of calibrations is in evidence, and the product associated with the pertinent instrument will not be shipped to the customer until the instrument in question is recalibrated and is found to be in-tolerance and properly recorded.)

Use of Outside Products and Services[13]

The director of quality assurance and the manager of metrology will support the purchasing manager when soliciting capable outside calibration sources. All purchase requisitions are reviewed by the metrology manager for adequacy and approved by the director of quality assurance. The purchasing department will assure that all delegated calibration system requirements are made known to the subcontractor or vendor. The purchase order will reflect a clear description of supplies and services including as appropriate:

- Specifications
- Drawings
- Calibration system requirements
- Requirements for qualification
- Calibration instructions
- Feedback data (reports/certifications)

An employee from the quality-control department conducts an on-site assessment of the proposed supplier's quality-assurance capabilities before a purchase order is issued for solicited instruments and/or calibration services under the following conditions: (a) the supplier did not achieve ANSI/ISO/ASQC certification and registration status, (b) there is no history in the company's files that indicates subcontractor/vendor capabilities, and (c) a supplier does not have an established reputation within the industry to indicate acceptable capabilities.

Storage and Handling[14]
Company-owned M&TE and MS

All instruments shall be stored, handled, and transported in such a manner as to protect them from damage, deterioration, wear, and calibration status. Active as well as out-of-service instruments will be stored in separate containers to protect them from physical damage. Each measuring surface shall be cleaned with a lint-free cloth prior to use. Surfaces shall be coated with a film of corrosion-resistant oil over areas requiring protection against rust when not in use. Where necessary, the instruments will be wrapped in moisture-free barrier material before they are placed in storage. Both company and customer-supplied M&TE shall be visually examined by the calibration technician and inspectors prior to use to detect out-of-tolerance conditions caused by improper handling or storage.

Customer–Supplied M&TE and MS

Customer-supplied instruments shall be examined upon receipt for corrosion or physical damage. Instruments found to be unserviceable for use will be recorded and reported to the customer. Instruments received in good condition will be handled and stored the same as company-owned instruments.

Traceability[15]

One of the fundamental requirements of our calibration system is to assure traceability of our M&TE and MS via an unbroken chain of calibrations to the National Institute of Standards and Technology (NIST) or, where appropriate, to an international standard. Since we do not do business directly with NIST, however, or any international laboratory, the company's focus will be centered on the independent laboratory that calibrates company standards. It is from these standards that the metrology department calibrates all working instruments. The director of purchasing, with support from the director of quality assurance, shall ensure that purchase orders that are issued to an independent laboratory contain the following feedback data:

- Required calibration system standard
- Item nomenclature
- Identification of the appropriate calibration system standards
- Certificate number
- NIST report number
- Date of calibration
- Identification of nominal characteristics checked

- Identification of measured values
- Areas of uncertainty
- Relevant conditions (environment under which stated values were obtained)
- Statement that calibrations were conducted with standards used to calibrate subcontracted instruments are traceable to a national or international standard
- Certification signature, title, and date of an authorized representative of the calibration laboratory

The metrology manager or his/her designated representative shall examine and validate certificates and/or reports associated with the calibrated instrument by applying his/her signature to the certificate/report before it is routed to the files. Files are held at least three years or as many years specified by the customer. Files are routed to the director of purchasing via the director of quality assurance for necessary action when the certificate/report is found to be nonconforming. Certificates or reports of calibration shall be kept readily accessible to internal and external customers. As part of an investigation regarding the traceability of a nonconforming product or service, the customer-complaint monitor and the owner of an associated process checks the quality plan to assure that specified technical requirements were properly addressed.

Environmental Controls[16]

Obtaining the accuracy of inspection, measuring, and test equipment within a controlled environment will be accomplished to the extent necessary in order to maintain detrimental conditions within acceptable limits of the calibration being performed. Where appropriate, adequate compensating corrections shall be made. In addition:

- Calibration stations shall be free from extraneous equipment and supplies.
- Storage and holding areas shall be kept in an orderly manner.
- Technicians must wipe measuring surfaces with a lint-free cloth or commercial paper wipe before each measurement.

- Benches and other calibration surfaces shall be sufficiently free from vibration so that readings can be consistently obtained to an accuracy of at least the value indicated for each reading.
- Relative humidity conditions shall range between 35 percent and 55 percent.
- Temperature conditions shall be maintained from 67.5° F to 68.5° F for reference standards and from 68° F to 73° F for working standards.
- Lighting shall be 80 foot-candles at bench tops.

PERSONNEL [17]
Management
The functions of calibration systems management are assigned to personnel who have achieved certification status from an accredited third party (see Figure 6.2).

Technicians
Calibration technicians will qualify to work within our metrology department after they have completed six-month internal training, or they must have at least five years experience in precision measurement with a previous employer or are certified by an accredited agency (see figure 6.2).

Documentation of metrology policy and procedures is an imperative for promoting a clear understanding of calibration systems requirements. This documentation helps to ensure that they are appropriately coordinated with personnel associated with quality systems in design, development, production, installation, and servicing.

Employee Training Record
(metrology)

Name _____ Date _____

Home address _____

1. Calibration capabilities

Discipline	Qualified			If yes, source of training		
	Yes	No	Certified	Formal	Previous employer
Mechanical __	__	__	__	__	__
Electrical	__	__	__	__	__
Electronic	__	__	__	__	__
Pneumatic	__	__	__	__	__
Hydraulic	__	__	__	__	__
Force	__	__	__	__	__

Certified mechanical inspector   Yes __   No __

Certified quality technician   Yes __   No __

2. Calibration systems management capabilities

Certified quality engineer   Yes __   No __

Certified reliability and maintainability engineer   Yes __   No __

Professional engineer in the discipline of quality   Yes __   No __

3. Required company training

			If no, scheduled training date
Policy procedures	Yes __	No __	_____
Calibration procedures	Yes __	No __	_____
Written processes	Yes __	No __	_____
Work instructions	Yes __	No __	_____
Intern program	Yes __	No __	_____

4. List of skills and years of experience

5. Future training plans

Training monitor

Figure 6.2   Record of employee training.

Notes

From ISO 10012-1, 1992, Quality Assurance Requirements for
   Measuring Equipment—Part 1: Metrological Confirmation
   System for Measuring Equipment.

1. Clause 4.3, 4.
2. Clause 4.5, 5.
3. Clause 4.4, 4.
4. Clause 4.2, 4.
5. Clause 4.6, 6.
6. Clause 4.16, 10.
7. Clause 4.7, 6.
8. Clause 4.8, 6.
9. Clause 4.9, 7.
10. Clause 4.10, 7.
11. Clause 4.12, 8.
12. Clause 4.11, 8.
13. Clause 4.13, 9.
14. Clause 4.14, 9.
15. Clause 4.15, 9.
16. Clause 4.17, 10.
17. Clause 4.18, 10.

CHAPTER 7

Costs Associated with Metrology Systems Management

Total quality costs is intended to represent the difference between the actual cost of a product or service and what the costs would be if the quality was perfect. It is, as previously ascribed to Juran, "gold in the mine," just waiting to be extracted. When you zero in on the elimination of failure costs and then challenge the level of appraisal costs, you will not only be managing the cost of quality, you will be mining gold.[1]

The control of quality costs is another option available to a product manufacturer or independent calibration laboratory for measuring the effectiveness of a metrology system. Two points of leverage can be attacked by metrology professionals in conjunction with management. These points can be found in the proper assessment of contract requirements and the monitoring of actions associated with 10 critical quality elements through the proper application of the procedures specified in the preceding chapters.

Basic to all cost control, credibility and customer service is the control of out-of-tolerance conditions, which focus the actions of the metrology professional.

EFFECTIVE USE OF THE CONTRACT OR TECHNICAL SPECIFICATIONS

When contract requirements are clearly defined and distributed in a timely fashion, it enhances the planning process between the procuring contracting officer's contract administrator and the prime contractor and it also leads to a cost-effective operation. As described in chapter 1, the contract and its associated drawings and documentation are fertile areas for the introduction of costly and compromising errors of omission. Clarity and a careful system for communicating specifications and work changes can dramatically affect profitability and the delivery of a quality product.

There are two places that the metrology professional can make use of the contract or technical specifications to avoid potentially unnecessary work or to be sure that the correct action is taken to avoid rework. These are the proper understanding of complexity and criticality and the proper application of intervals of calibration. Either of these factors may or may not be specified in the contract or technical specifications. It is important for the metrology professional to have a clear idea regarding which standards are to be applied and to have a clear rationale for their application. The decision to apply complexity versus criticality or to make decisions regarding intervals of calibration influences cost as well as the validity of the calibration system.

Complexity Versus Criticality

Complex items have quality characteristics, not wholly visible in the end item, for which contractual conformance must be established progressively through precise measurements, tests, and controls applied during purchasing, manufacturing, performance, assembly, and functional operation either as an individual item or in conjunction with other items. Noncomplex items have quality characteristics for which simple measurements and tests of the end item are sufficient to determine conformance to contractual requirements.[2]

A critical application of an item is one in which failure of the item could injure personnel or jeopardize a vital mission. A critical item may be either peculiar, meaning it has only one application, or common, meaning it has multiple applications. A noncritical application is any other application. Noncritical items may also be peculiar or common.[3]

Products associated with a complex product design require an extensive and diversified amount of measuring instruments and therefore present many opportunities to improve the processes and procedures associated with metrology systems management.

A critical application of a product is normally associated with items that are classified as complex.

An Aircraft Flight Recorder and Naval Radar Systems are two examples of complex/critical items. Each requires a sophisticated amount of measuring equipment to check their component parts, subassemblies, and functional testing of the end item, and they are critical to an assigned mission as well as for protecting the safety and lives of personnel who use them.

Intervals of Calibration

One of the most promising areas for cost savings in the metrology system is in the establishment, application, and maintenance of objective calibration intervals.

There are no restrictions placed on metrology managers as to what methodology is employed when establishing an interval of calibration that satisfactorily meets a reliability target or how a calibration interval is adjusted if the desired reliability is not being met. Specific intervals of calibration for inspection, measuring, and test equipment and MS may be established contractually by a calibration laboratory that is located in the manufacturer's facility or by an independent calibration laboratory. Whatever source is selected, the supplier of the metrology service must demonstrate that each instrument is calibrated and traceable of objective quality evidence.

Impact of Out-of-Tolerance Conditions

When significant out-of-tolerance conditions (see chapter 2) prevail, it adds costs to the bottom line that were not anticipated during the preparation of an original quality plan such as:

1. Costs associated with instruments found to be significantly out-of-tolerance will involve investigation and appropriate corrective action at all internal and external calibration stations where the instruments in question were calibrated or used.

2. Lost person hours to verify the accuracy of M&TE and to reinspect products that were inspected during in-process as well as final inspection operations.

3. Where a contact stipulates that final inspection and acceptance shall be at destination costs incurred for this function are absorbed by the prime contractor. Where the product is found to be defective, however, associated costs to screen, cull, repair, reject, or replace the product is usually absorbed by the product manufacturer.

4. Costs increase for processing a request for waiver regarding a product deficiency that does not adversely impact form, fit, or function.

5. Expenses occur when determining if products shipped to the customer do not comply with contractual requirements.

6. Costs are realized to review/upgrade and, where appropriate, prepare new calibration procedures.

Impact of In-Tolerance Conditions

In-tolerance conditions that are supported with objective quality evidence provide quality-systems managers with information that will

- Justify a decision to lengthen a calibration interval and therefore reduce costs to calibrate instruments
- Share cost savings with the customer with subsequent procurements where the cost saving is significant over an extended period of time
- Reduce the supplier's risk of producing nonconforming products
- Reduce the purchaser's risk of receiving nonconforming products

Suppliers of products and services are cautioned not to calibrate inspection, measuring, and test equipment at an established interval for an extended period of time without taking advantage of the opportunity that is presented to them when documented calibration data allows the using activity to lengthen an interval of calibration and at the same time save time and money without compromising instrument accuracy. Some suppliers have an attitude of, "Why should I get involved with changing calibration intervals when I know that my instruments are accurate and reliable every time we calibrate them?" This perception is not in consonance with a cost-effective operation, because every time a calibration interval is justifiably lengthened there is a reduction of labor hours as well as reduction of costs to calibrate inspection, measuring, and test equipment. Conversely, when calibration records conclusively indicate a significant out-of-tolerance condition, intervals of calibration will normally have to be shortened and costs to calibrate will escalate. Figures 7.1 through 7.4 that follow are intended to show how costs to calibrate are reduced when an interval of calibration is justifiably lengthened and how unanticipated costs to calibrate are added to the bottom line when an interval of calibration is shortened.*

Factors
- Duration to calibration of one instrument (DCOI)
- Hourly rate of the technician (HRT)
- Calibration interval (CI)
- Number of like instruments (NLI)

----

*Figures 7.1 through 7.4 are intended to show comparison costs when a calibration interval is changed. It is not to imply that all changes can be made in the same calendar year, but rather, to show the comparison that interval changes have on costs to calibrate when intervals are lengthened or shortened over a certain period of time. The figures pertain to one instrument; however, cost savings can be further appreciated when there are two or more like instruments with the same accuracy requirements and the same calibration interval and where an interval of calibration is justifiably lengthened.

Formula: NLI × DCOI × HRT × CI = Yearly costs to calibrate M&TE

Factors:

CI = Various (see table below)

NLI = 1

DCOI = 2 hours

HRT = $20.00

$$NLI \times DCOI \times HRT \times CI$$
$$= 1 \times 2 \times 20 \times 12$$
$$= \$480$$

DCOI = 2 hours
HRT = $20.00

Comparison of yearly costs to calibrate one instrument when intervals are lengthened

Number of like items	Calibration interval*	Number of yearly calibrations	Required man-hours	Yearly cost to calibrate
1	1	12.0	24.0	$480
1	2	6.0	12.0	240
1	3	4.0	8.0	160
1	4	3.0	6.0	120
1	5	2.4	4.8	96
1	6	2.0	4.0	80
1	7	1.7	3.4	68
1	8	1.5	3.0	60
1	9	1.3	2.6	52
1	10	1.2	2.4	48
1	11	1.09	2.18	44
1	12	1.0	1.0	20

*Monthly

Figure 7.1   Impact of lengthened calibration intervals.

EFFECTIVE USE OF CALIBRATION INTERVALS

Savvy metrology managers recognize that the establishment of calibration intervals is an area where costs to calibrate inspection, measuring, and test equipment can escalate. This escalation generally occurs when proper consideration is not given to the degree of usage, instrument accuracy, type of standard or

Comparison of monthly costs to calibrate one instrument when intervals are lengthened

Interval frequency	Months												Number of yearly intervals
	1	2	3	4	5	6	7	8	9	10	11	12	
1-	100	x	x	x	x	x	x	x	x	x	x	x	12.0
2-		50	–	x	–	x	–	x	–	x	–	x	6.0
3-			33.3	–	–	x	–	–	x	–	–	x	4.0
4-				25	–	–	–	x	–	–	–	x	3.0
5-					20	–	–	–	–	x	–	–	2.4
6-						16.7	–	–	–	–	–	x	2.0
7-							14.2	–	–	–	–	–	1.7
8-								12.5	–	–	–	–	1.5
9-									11	–	–	x	1.3
10-										10.8	–	–	1.2
11-											9.2	–	1.1
12-												8.3	1.0

Percent

Figure 7.2   Percent of yearly costs when intervals are lengthened.

equipment, required precision, and other conditions that adversely affect the measurement process, such as the environment in which an instrument is processed. Effective managers also recognize that when data associated with an established calibration interval is periodically reviewed and intervals are adjusted accordingly (lengthened or shortened) reliability targets will be met and a positive impact on quality costs will be present. These managers continuously monitor (see chapter 3) items that reduce cost escalation while contributing to the delivery of a quality product. For example:

- Calibration intervals are adequate to provide required confidence regarding instrument accuracy.
- Inspection-department personnel are prohibited from using inspection, measuring, and test equipment past their calibration due date without referring the matter for preliminary assessment to a material review board for adjudication (see chapter 5).

	DOCI = 2 Hours		
	HRT = $20.00		
	(One Item)		

Comparison of yearly costs to calibrate one instrument when intervals are shortened

Interval frequency*	Number of yearly calibrations	Required man-hours	Yearly cost to calibrate
12	1.0	1.0	$20
11	1.09	2.18	44
10	2.1	2.4	48
9	1.3	2.6	52
8	1.5	3.0	60
7	1.7	3.4	58
6	2.0	4.0	80
5	2.4	4.8	96
4	3.0	6.0	120
3	4.0	8.0	160
2	6.0	12.0	240
1	12.0	24.0	480

*Monthly

Figure 7.3   Impact of shortened calibration intervals.

Comparison of monthly costs to calibrate one instrument when intervals are shortened

Interval frequency	Months												Number of yearly intervals
	1	2	3	4	5	6	7	8	9	10	11	12	
12–												8.3	1.0
11–											9.2	–	1.1
10–										10	–	–	1.2
9–									10.8	–	–	–	1.3
8–								12.5	–	–	–	–	1.5
7–							14.2	–	–	–	–	–	1.7
6–						16.7	–	–	–	–	–	x	2.0
5–					20	–	–	–	–	x	–	x	2.4
4–				25	–	–	–	x	–	–	–	x	3.0
3–			33.3	–	–	x	–	–	x	–	–	x	4.0
2–		50	–	x	–	x	–	x	–	x	–	x	6.0
1–	100	x	x	x	x	x	x	x	x	x	x	x	12.0

| | 1 | 2 | 3 | 4 | 5 | 6 | 7 | 8 | 9 | 10 | 11 | 12 | |

Percent

Figure 7.4   Percent of yearly costs when intervals are shortened.

- Inspection departments are prohibited from using inspection, measuring, and test equipment past their due date for calibration without permission granted to the supplier from its customer. Such cases carry the proviso that the instrument(s) in question is to be recalibrated for accuracy before the applicable production lot is shipped from the supplier's shipping department or to its next destination within the company.

As in all good business, good judgment is an important part of any process. Experience has shown that suppliers can, at times, also add unnecessary costs to the bottom line through "overkill." Even though data analysis and recalibrations indicate stability and accuracy of inspection, measuring, and test equipment, the supplier elects not to shorten a calibration interval where such action may be quite appropriate. For example:

- Calibrates daily where weekly is acceptable
- Calibrates weekly where monthly is acceptable
- Calibrates instruments on an established calibration interval where the prior-to-use method is more appropriate

The intelligent, documented, and applied methods for decisions regarding intervals of calibration produce the desired objective for the metrology professional; that is, controlling unnecessary costs while producing a product that is free of defect.

TEN-ELEMENT CHECKLIST

Ten critical elements of a metrology system and related factors that have a direct impact on the costs associated with the establishment, implementation, and maintenance of a calibration system are listed on the following pages. The list is designed to be a practical, working tool to bring the metrology system together, joining efficiency with effectiveness. The checklist should be used by management and operations to self-evaluate the organization and its relevant vendors in order to hold the system accountable. Try using the checklist to examine current capabilities and needs. It should serve as a catalyst for improvement goals and for the recognition and on-going monitoring of achievement.

1. *Personnel*   Factors include:
- Metrology management personnel are consistently familiar with detail and contractual requirements and associated drawings, specifications, and standards.
- Personnel performing calibration systems management have defined responsibility, authority, and organizational freedom to identify and evaluate metrology problems.
- Employees are encouraged to provide suggestions and recommendations that will improve established calibration policies, procedures, and associated processes.
- Employees receive ongoing training regarding the application of complex procedures and work instructions.
- Supplier assures that there is clear communication of contract and technical requirements at all levels of metrology management.
- Supplier assures that qualified personnel are on hand to administer the metrology program.
- Supplier identifies training needs of its metrology management personnel and provides timely training to its personnel where required.

2. *Quality plan*   Factors include:
- A written quality plan exists.
- The plan is capable of addressing all of the technical requirements specified in a contractual agreement between two parties or a system for handling exceptions is in place.
- The plan addresses requirements for special inspection and test equipment, tooling, and skills.
- The quality plan addresses tailored specification requirements that have a direct bearing on the selection of special inspection and test equipment.
- The plan provides procedures for comparing new contract or purchase order requirements with previously prepared metrology procedures and processes and for making changes where appropriate.

- The plan addresses the need for acquiring new facilities and inspection and measuring equipment, when required.
- Work instructions referenced in the plan are consistently defined and are all-inclusive.
- The plan describes the method for recording calibration measurements (variable and/or attributes data).
- The plan defines the acceptable environmental conditions under which calibration measurements are taken and identifies the method for identifying these conditions.
- Supplier assures that the customer's prescribed calibration system is compatible with products and services offered.
- Supplier's established procedures provide for the adequacy, currentness, and completeness of tailored specifications, processes, or work instructions related to the metrology program.

3. *Control of documentation*   Factors include:
   - Procedures for documenting the adequacy, completeness, and currentness of drawings, specifications, and standards are in place.
   - The control of design changes that impact the metrology system are documented.
   - The effective point of contract notices associated with metrology requirements are identified.
   - Superseded documents that impact the performance of inspection, measuring, and test equipment are removed from the production area.
   - Changes to drawing and/or specification and associated documentation that impact the metrology system are furnished to the prime contractor's designated subcontractors.
   - Documented metrology data is reviewed by management for reliability and improvement on a regularly scheduled basis.
   - Documented calibration inspection records are reviewed and analyzed to identify problem areas.

- Responsibility and schedule for review are explicit.
- Supplier documents an individual record for each measuring instrument and measurement standard that addresses
  a. A description and identification of measuring equipment
  b. Calibration interval
  c. Calibrated due date
  d. Identification of calibration source
  e. Calibration procedure
  f. Calibration results
  g. Out of tolerance conditions
  h. Compensating correction of measurements (where appropriate)

4. *Control of inspection, measuring, and test equipment*   Factors include:
   - The supplier recognizes that a 4:1 or higher accuracy level between inspection and measuring equipment and the product characteristic is an imperative for checking product quality.
   - The supplier recognizes that a 10:1 accuracy level or higher between measurement standards and working measuring and test equipment is an important element of a calibration procedure.
   - Accuracy ratios between measurement standards and working gages always kept within acceptable areas of acceptance.
   - Significant out-of-tolerance condition levels are identified.
   - Calibration intervals are predicated on the degree of usage or as designated in a contractual agreement between purchaser and supplier.
   - Calibration procedures are revised where appropriate and new calibration procedures are prepared when needed.
   - Capability of new providers of metrology services is verified before a purchase order is issued.

- A procedure for the handling and storage of measuring instruments to assure that accuracies are maintained is established and followed consistently.
- M&TE that are used to verify that supplies conform to contract quality requirements are adequately maintained and controlled in accordance with specified requirements.
- The accuracy of M&TE is verified against a certified measurement standard.
- The prime contractor verifies subcontractor calibration system capabilities.
- The calibration system is coordinated with other quality-assurance systems where it impacts the accuracy of M&TE and measurement standards.
- M&TE is properly handled, stored, transported, and protected from corrosion.
- M&TE and MS are labeled to indicate calibration status.
- Measuring instruments are calibrated to their full capability.
- Measuring instruments having limitations of use are labeled or limitations are identified.
- Instructions for the use of tamper-resistant seals and disposition of items whose seals are broken are provided.

5. *Nonconforming products and services*   Factors include:
   - An effective system for controlling nonconforming material, which includes procedures for identification, segregation, and disposition of nonconforming products and metrology services, is in place.
   - Procedures provide for the positive identification of nonconforming M&TE.
   - Nonconforming products are reworked and measuring instruments are repaired using documented procedures that are acceptable to both internal and external customers.
   - Nonconforming M&TE are processed via preliminary review and, where necessary, via a material review board.
   - A report of cost associated with the scrap and rework of products attributed out-of-tolerance M&TE is supplier-maintained and provided to the metrology manager.

6. *Corrective action*   Factors include:
- A documented corrective action procedure is in place.
- Causes of deficiencies attributed to out-of-tolerance M&TE are eliminated.
- Prime contractor assures that subcontractors recalibrate M&TE that is found to be out-of-tolerance.
- Procedures associated with nonconforming products and services include a requirement for the investigation of metrology procedures, measuring equipment that was used to inspect the product, and related calibration data to determine
  a. The impact on products previously produced
  b. The need for employee training
  c. The prevention of subsequent nonconforming products or services
  d. The need to improve established procedures and work instructions
  e. The identification of required corrective action
  f. The effectiveness of corrective action taken

7. *Control of purchases*   Factors include:
- An ongoing assessment of M&TE of supplier's quality data is conducted to verify product and service quality.
- Effectiveness, integrity, and control of measuring instruments used by subcontractors is monitored at intervals consistent with the complexity of the end item.
- Metrology test reports, certificates, and other suitable evidence furnished by an independent calibration laboratory are monitored and evaluated to assure that services are provided in accordance with purchase agreements.

8. *Customer-supplied products*   Factors include:
- Product and/or measuring instruments are examined upon receipt to detect any functional damage related to poor transportation or handling.
- Periodic inspection of stored M&TE is conducted to assure adequate protection from damage.

- Measuring surfaces are preserved and protected from corrosion.
- The organization (customer or supplier) responsible for recalibration and maintenance of instrument accuracy is clearly identified.

9. *Inspection and testing*   Factors include:
   - Inspection and testing records are traceable to M&TE that are used to check product characteristics and they are available for review by internal and external auditors.
   - Reported product deficiencies and associated out-of-tolerance measuring equipment are submitted for preliminary review or, where appropriate, for assessment by a material review board.
   - Supplier assures that calibration system requirements that are delegated to subcontractors are not under- or over-specified. Note: The purchaser should be careful not to fall into the trap of duplicating metrology systems management delegated to the subcontractor.

10. *Quality audits*   Factors include:
    - Supplier conducts scheduled and unscheduled metrology audits.
    - Supplier has a documented metrology audit procedure in place.
    - Metrology audit schedules are documented and supported with a "tickler" file.
    - Metrology audits are performed by a second or third party not involved in the processes audited.
    - Top management reviews audit reports and provides proactive recommendations.
    - The supplier assures that metrology audits are not performed by the "owners" of the process

Costs incurred during the use and maintenance of inspection, measuring, and test equipment associated with a noncomplex/noncritical product design such as an off-the-shelf item are minimal compared with the costs that are required to produce higher-level complex/critical items. Areas that present opportunities to reduce costs include:

- Rental costs for specialized (cost-effective) M&TE
- Development of new calibration procedures, processes, work instructions, and techniques
- Trips to subcontractor's facility to assess capabilities and efficiencies regarding the use and calibration of specialized M&TE
- The acquisition of more efficient plant facilities and equipment

Notes

1. Principles of quality costs. 1990. *Principles, Implementation, and Use* 2d ed. Milwaukee: ASQC Quality Press.
2. U.S. Department of Defense, General Services Administration, and National Aeronautics and Space Agency, *Federal Acquisition Regulation (FAR)*, 1995, Part 46, Clause 46.203(b).
3. *FAR*, 1993, Part 46, Clause 46.203(c).

GLOSSARY

Accuracy   The closeness of agreement between an observed value and an accepted reference value. (1)

Auditee   The organization being audited. (2)

Calibration   The set of operations that established, under specified conditions, the relationship between values indicated by a measuring instrument or measuring system, or values represented by a material measure or a reference material, and the corresponding values of a quantity realized by a reference standard. (3)

Characteristic   A property that helps to differentiate between items of a given sample population. Note: The differentiation may be either quantitative (by variables) or qualitative (by attributes). (1)

Comparator   An instrument for comparing some measurement with a fixed standard. (5)

Conformity   Fulfillment of specified requirements. (2)

Contract review   Systematic activities carried out by the supplier before signing the contract to ensure that requirements for quality are adequately defined, free from ambiguity, documented, and can be realized by the supplier. (2)

Contractor   Supplier in a contractual situation. (2)

Corrective action   Action taken to eliminate the causes of an existing nonconformity defect or other undesirable situation in order to prevent recurrence. (2)

Customer   Recipient of a product provided by the supplier. (2)

Defect   Nonfulfillment of an intended usage requirement of reasonable expectation, including one concerned with safety. (2)

Degree of documentation   Extent to which evidence is produced to provide confidence that specified requirements are fulfilled. (2)

Disposition of nonconformity   Action to be taken to deal with an existing nonconforming entity in order to resolve the nonconformity. (2)

Element   A quality of product, material, or service forming a cohesive entity on which a measurement or observation may be made. (1)

Hold point   Point defined in an appropriate document, beyond which an activity must not proceed without the approval of a designated organization or authority. (2)

Inspection   The process of measuring, examining, testing, gaging, or otherwise comparing the unit with the applicable requirements. (1)

Inspection by attributes   Inspection by attribute is inspection whereby either the unit of product is classified as conforming or nonconforming, or the number of nonconformities in the product is counted, with respect to a given requirement or a set of requirements. (4)

Item   An object or quantity of material on which a set of observations can be made. Or, the result of making an observation of an object or quantity of material. (1)

Management review   Formal evaluation by top management of the status and adequacy of the quality system in relation to quality policy and objectives. (2)

Measurement standards (MS)   A material measure, measuring instrument, reference material, or system intended to define, conserve, or reproduce a unit or one or more values of a quantity in order to transmit them to other measuring instruments by comparison. (3)

Measuring equipment   All of the measuring instruments, measurement standards, reference materials, auxiliary apparatus, and instructions that are necessary to carry out a measurement. This includes measuring equipment used in the course of that used in calibration. (3)

Metrology   The science of measurements. (5)

Model for quality assurance   Standardized or selected set of quality system requirements situation. (2)

Nonconformity   Nonfulfillment of a specified requirement. (2)

Objective evidence   Information that can be proved true, based on facts obtained through observation, measurement, tests or other means. (2)

Organization   Company, corporation, firm, enterprise, or institution or part, thereof, whether incorporated or not, public or private, that has its own functions and administration. (2)

Organizational structure   Responsibilities, authorities, and relationships, arranged in a pattern, through which an organization performs its functions. (2)

Precision   The closeness of agreement between randomly selected individual measurements or test results. (1)

Preventive action   Action taken to eliminate the causes of a potential nonconformity defect or other undesirable situation in order to prevent recurrence. (2)

Purchaser   Customer in a contractual situation. (2)

Qualification process   Process of demonstrating whether an entity is capable of fulfilling specified requirements. (2)

Qualified   Status given to an entity when capability of fulfilling specified requirements has been demonstrated. (2)

Quality   The totality of features and characteristics of a product or service that bears on its ability to satisfy given needs. (1)

Quality assurance   All those planned or systematic actions necessary to provide adequate confidence that a product or service will satisfy given needs. (1)

Quality audit   A systematic and independent examination to determine whether quality activities and related results comply with planned arrangements and whether these arrangements are implemented effectively and are suitable to achieve objectives. (3)

Quality audit observation   Statement of fact during a quality audit and substantiated by objective evidence. (2)

Quality auditor   Person qualified to perform quality audits. (2)

Quality control   The operational techniques and the activities that sustain a quality of product or service that will satisfy given needs; also, the use of such techniques and activities. (1)

Quality evaluation   Systematic examination of the extent to which an entity is capable of fulfilling specified requirements (2)

Quality losses   Losses caused by not realizing the potential of resources in processes and activities. (2)

Quality management   The totality of functions involved in the determination and achievement of quality. (1)

Quality manual   Document stating the quality policy and describing the quality system of an organization. (2)

Quality plan   Document setting out the specific quality practices, resources, and sequence of activities relevant to a particular product, project, or contract. (2)

Quality policy   Overall intentions and direction of an organization with regard to quality, as formally expressed by top management. (2)

Quality-related costs   Those costs incurred in ensuring satisfactory quality, as well as the losses incurred when satisfactory quality is not achieved. (2)

Quality surveillance   Continued monitoring and verification of the status of an entity and analysis of records to ensure that specification requirements are being fulfilled. (2)

Quality system   Organizational structure procedures, processes, and resources needed to implement quality management. (2)

Requirement for quality   Expression of the needs or their translation into a set of quantitatively or qualitatively stated requirements for the characteristics of an entity to enable its realization and examination. (2)

Specification   Document stating requirements. (2)

Subcontractor   Organization that provides a product to the supplier. (2)

Supplier   Organization that provides a product to a customer. (2)

Testing   A means of determining the capability of an item to meet specified requirements by subjecting the item to a set of physical, chemical, environmental, or operation actions and conditions. (1)

Total quality management   Management approach of an organization, centered on quality based on the participation of its members and aiming at long-term success through customer satisfaction and benefits of all members of the organization and to society. (2)

Traceability   Ability to trace the history, application, or location of an entity by means of recorded identification. (2)

Uncertainty   An indication of the variability associated with a measured value that takes into account two major components of error: (1) bias and (2) the random error attributed to the impression of the measurement process. (1)

Unit   A quantity of product, material, or service forming a cohesive entity on which a measurement or observation may be made. (1)

Variables, method of   Measurement of quality by measuring and recording the numerical magnitude of a quality characteristic for each of the units in the group under consideration. This involves reference to a continuous scale of some kind. (1)

Verification   Confirmation by examination and provision of objective evidence that specified requirements have been filled. (2)

Source for glossary terms

(1) American Society for Quality Control. 1983. *Glossary and Tables for Statistical Quality Control.* 2d ed.

(2) ISO 8402, 1994 International Standard, Quality Management and Quality Assurance—Vocabulary.

(3) ISO 10012-1, 1992 International Standard, Quality Assurance Requirements for Measuring Equipment.

(4) ANSI/ASQC Z1.4, 1993 American National Standard, Sampling Procedures and Tables for Inspection by Attributes.

(5) *Webster's New World Dictionary of the American Language.* 1975. Springfield: G&C Merriam Co.

ACRONYMS

ANSI	American National Standards Institute
ASQC	American Society for Quality Control
CEO	Chief executive officer
CI	Calibration interval
CP	Calibration procedure
FOB	Free on board
GIDEP	Government and Industry Data Exchange Program
HRT	Hourly rate of technician
ISO	International Organization for Standardization
IEC	International Electrotechnical Commission
M&TE	Measuring and test equipment
M&TAT	Measuring and test equipment accuracy tolerance
MRB	Material review board
MS	Measurement standard
NCSL	National Conference of Standards Laboratories
NIST	National Institute of Standards and Technology
NLI	Number of like items
PAT	Primary standard accuracy tolerance
PR	Preliminary review
PSIG	Pounds-per-square-inch gage
R	Ratio
SAT	Secondary standard accuracy tolerance
TQM	Total quality management

BIBLIOGRAPHY

American Society for Quality Control. *Statistics Glossary and Tables for Statistical Quality Control.* 2d ed, 1983.

ANSI/ASQC MI. American National Standard for Calibration Systems, 1987.

ANSI/ASQC Z1 4. Sampling Procedures and Tables for Inspection by Attributes, 1993.

ANSI/ASQC Z540-1. American National Standard for Calibration. Calibration Laboratories and Measuring and Test Equipment—General Requirements.

ANSI/ISO/ASQC. 10011 Guidelines for Auditing Quality Systems, 1994.

ANSI/ISO/ASQC Q9000-1. Quality Management and Quality Assurance—Guidelines for Selection and Use, 1994.

ANSI/ISO/ASQC Q9001. Quality Systems—Model for Quality Assurance in Design, Development, Production, Installation, and Servicing, 1994.

ANSI/ISO/ASQC Q9002. Quality Systems—Model for Quality Assurance in Production, Installation, and Servicing, 1994.

ANSI/ISO/ASQC Q9003. Quality Systems—Model for Quality Assurance in Final Inspection, 1994.

ANSI/ISO/ASQC Q10011. American Equivalent of the International Organization for Standardization—Department of Defense Evaluation of a Contractor's Calibration System Handbook MIL-HDBK 52, August, 1989.

Campanella, Jack. *Principles of Quality Costs: Principles, Implementation, and Use,* 2d ed. Milwaukee: ASQC Quality Press, 1990.

155

Chrysler/Ford/General Motors Supply Quality Requirements Task Force. Quality System Requirements QS-9000, 1995.

Department of Defense. Mil-Std 120 Gage Inspection, September, 1963.

Department of Defense and National Aeronautics and Space Agency. DoD/NASA-HDBK Q9000, 1994.

Department of Defense, Calibration System Requirements Mil-Std 45662A, August, 1988.

Department of Defense, General Services Administration, and National Aeronautics and Space Administration. Government Federal Acquisition Regulation, March 1995.

Griffith, Gary. *Quality Technician's Technical Handbook.* New York: John Wiley and Sons, Inc., 1986.

International Organization for Standardization. ISO/IEC Guide 25: General Requirements for the Competence of Calibration and Testing Laboratories, 1990.

International Organization for Standardization. ISO 10012-1, Quality Assurance Requirements for Measuring Equipment— Part 1: Metrological Confirmation System for Measuring Equipment, 1992.

International Organization for Standardization. ISO 8402 International Standard. Quality Management and Quality Assurance Vocabulary, 1994.

INDEX